دموع إبراهيم

ABRAHAM'S TEARS

דמעות של אברהם

دموع إبراهيم

ABRAHAM'S TEARS
דמעות של אברהם

A Palestinian-Israeli Tragedy

or

How a Muslim and Jew
Came Together to Work for
Middle East Peace

Bruce Stein

Kalamazoo Publishing
2012

© 2012 Bruce Stein
All rights reserved

No part of this publication may be reproduced, stored in a retrieval system, or transmitted in any form or by any means, electronic, mechanical, photocopying, recording, scanning, or otherwise, except as permitted under Section 107 or 108 of the 1976 United States Copyright Act, without prior written permission of the publisher.

Stein, Bruce
    Abraham's tears: A Palestinian-Israeli tragedy or how a Muslim and Jew came together to work for Middle East peace. Kalamazoo, Mich.: Kalamazoo Publishing, 2012.
xii, 230 p.
    I. Title 1. Peace-building—Middle East—Fiction 2. OneVoice (Organization)

ISBN 978-0-9831991-1-3

Book layout: Words by Design
Kalamazoo, Michigan

Kalamazoo Publishing, LLC
Kalamazoo, Michigan, U.S.A
www.kazoopub.com

DEDICATION

Half a century ago when I was a child and listening to the news on the radio, there was fighting in the Middle East. I thought there was not much land to fight about, certainly both sides would find a way to settle their differences and jointly make the land flourish to support all ethnic and religious groups. Wrong. Since then, generation after generation on both sides has experienced untold suffering, has been involved in the same tit for tat killing, and we are back at square one.

This novel is dedicated to the memory of those who have died or been maimed in the Middle East fighting whether Israeli or Palestinian, whether Jew, Muslim or Christian.

In addition, it honors all those who have endured through the suicide bombings, shellings, military attacks, bombings, jailings and the day-to-day horrors of life, and still are working for a peaceful two-state solution. Further, it is written in the hope that maybe it can move the Middle East peace process one step closer to a peaceful resolution. If so, it will have been worth the time and effort.

How good and pleasant it is for everyone to live in unity.
— Psalms 133:1

We have created you male and female, and have made you nations and tribes that ye may know one another.
— Qur'an 49:13

An eye for an eye only ends up making the whole world blind.
— Mohandas Gandhi

CONTENTS

واحد	The Beginning of a Long Journey	1
שתים	A Young Man's Start	7
Three	Church Raffle	13
Vier	New Business	15
خمسة	Decisions, Decisions	17
שש	Planning Ahead	21
Seven	Selling Tickets	31
Acht	A Letter	33
تسعة	A Long Way from Home	35
עשר	A Different Path	45
Eleven	Notifying Sisters	51
Zwölf	Mixing Business with Pleasure?	53
ثلاثة عشر	It Can't Be	55
ארבע עשרה	Training Expands	63
Fifteen	Elizabeth's Reply	69

Sechzehn	An Atheist Going to Israel?	71
سبعة عشر	Eeny, Meeny, Miney, Moe	73
שמונה עשרה	Trouble	79
Nineteen	Ella's Reply	87
Zwanzig	Scheduling	89
واحد وعشرون	Vacation?	91
עשרים ושתיים	Going to Help My Sister	109
Twenty-three	And The Winner Is . . .	113
Vierundzwanzig	Travel Is August 8th	115
خمسة وعشرون	Israeli–Arab Conflict—Analyzed	117
עשרים ושש	Surprise	129
Twenty-seven	Notifying Elizabeth	137
Achtundzwanzig	Meeting on August 9th	139
تسعة وعشرون	The Answer	141
שלושים	The How and Why	151
Thirty-one	Problem	165
Zweiundreißig	Travel Details	167
ثلاثة وثلاثون	Oh, Brother	169
שלושים וארבע	A Busy Summer	173
Thirty-five	Planning Holy Land Trip	181
Sechsunddreißig	Flight Canceled	183
ثلاثون وسبعة و	Meeting Family	185
שלושים ושמונה	Meeting Dad	199

Thirty-nine	Bye	205
Vierzig	Take Bus #81	207
واحد وأربعون ארבעים ואחד Forty-one Einundvierzig	Tragedy	209
אפילוג خاتمة Epilogue Epilog	Epilogue	215

Acknowledgments ... 221

Author's Note ... 223

Abraham's Tears

واحد
THE BEGINNING OF A LONG JOURNEY

"The only way for the Jews and Arabs to peacefully coexist in the Middle East is for there to be two states," Samira replied for the thousandth time.

"If the Israelis wanted two states, they would withdraw from Palestine so we could have a country of our own. They don't want peace, they want to drive us out and have all the land!" her brother, Jamil, shot back.

"I think Israelis do want peace," said Samira. "It's the Palestinians that don't. Look at all the suicide bombers."

"Look at how Israel keeps occupying Palestinian land. There's never going to be peace this way."

"But there could be."

"Baloney!" said Jamil, "if we don't resist, they'll take everything."

"Come on, Jamil, if the Israelis really wanted to take all of Palestine's land, you know they would have done it by now. This stuff has been going on since before mom was born."

"Give me a break! They don't need an excuse. You know that in 1948 they took more than the UN Partition Plan allotted. Again in 1967 they took even more. We can't trust them. They break agreements. You know how little we trust the Sunnis, so you know I much I trust the Israelis."

"Don't use the term 'we' it's you who distrust the Sunnis. They are our brothers."

"Right! And you probably would have me believe because of Abraham, The Israelis are 'family.'"

They are at it again, thought Fatima Mansour as she rolled over trying to sleep. They have argued this so many times that by now even I know the script by heart. She hoped for a break in the conversation so she could fall sleep. Thankfully, the quiet peace which came from worthy opponents who realized they could not prevail permitted Fatima a window of time to enter the world of escaping dreams.

The next day, August 23rd, would be filled with work and then a drive to Michigan State to drop off Jamil. As the alarm went off, Fatima woke from a restless sleep, images of her son as a child. Scenes from when the family lived in the West Bank area when Jamil was only three had filled her dreams.

When there was some sort of disturbance like shooting or shelling, he would wander out of the house to see what was making the noise. No matter what she and her husband told him, out he would go; he needed looking after. She smiled, now he was 19 years old, 5'10", well-built and going back to college for his second year, and even though he could easily take care of himself, "mom" still wanted to do whatever she could to help him.

Three-thirty was too early to rise, long before the roosters squawked to wake the sun and tell it to bring light to the world for another day. Charlie, the Mansour family's calico cat, was also awakened by the alarm and he hopped up on to her bed to join Fatima in welcoming the day. Outside her window the streets were still, and last night's arguments from down the hall were silenced for the time being.

Being willing to work early earned Fatima an excellent job managing the bakery at Meijer in Allen Park, Michigan, which was very close to Dearborn, where her family lived. She was well aware it was very unusual in 1998 for a single Arab mother to manage a bakery of a large chain in a Detroit suburb. She had worked hard and persistently working her way up in the company over the years.

While she was not pleased by the continuous arguing of her kids, she was proud that they were interested in the real world issues affecting Arabs and Muslims.

Since she did not see her children until much later in the day, she always left them notes. Today she wrote to Jamil, are your clothes clean for school? Did you pack washing detergent for laundry? Do you want to take an umbrella? Are you sure all of your scholarship applications are in?

As she dressed and then headed off to the bakery, she could not help but reflect on her son's accomplishments. She felt it was obnoxious to talk with other mothers about all of these things, and relished the time that she had alone in the car when she could enjoy all of what both her children had done so far in their short lives.

When Jamil was in high school he was aware that his mother would never be able to afford to send both he and his sister to college, even if both went to an "in state" school. Hence, he realized two important things.

First, he needed to obtain as many scholarships as possible and to do that he realized the critical factor was grades in college prep courses. He studied very diligently, took a number of AP courses and received exemplary grades. He continued his diligent studying at MSU with similarly excellent results, having made the Dean's list each semester.

Secondly, he knew he needed to work to save money. During high school it was easy to find jobs at fast-food joints when he was not working at a carpet company owned by his best friend's father. The man, a fellow Arab, looked after other Arabs in the community who needed help. Because of his experience being employed by fast food places, when he entered MSU he was able to qualify for a job in a fraternity dining hall. It gave him free meals with good food which greatly helped his mother's budget. The down side was he had less time to study.

Jamil decided to major in biology because he knew it would be easier to find a job if he stayed in the States. If he decided to go back to Palestine, as he and his sister had dual citizenship, he would assist his Arab brothers to improve their farming and quality of life.

As Fatima continued her commute, she shifted her focus to her daughter, a senior at Crestwood High School in Dearborn Heights. Even though Samira was two years younger than Jamil, Fatima thought she was as mature in many ways. Fatima had a warm feeling as she reflected on how she had confidence in her daughter's ability to handle what came up and to look after herself including holding her own in arguments with her brother.

This was a particularly intense drive to work for Fatima. Because she had woken this morning feeling nostalgic for her life in the West Bank, she could not help her mind now wandering to the fates of her husband, her sister and sister's husband, all of whom were tragically killed in a cross-fire between Israeli forces and Palestinian militia. The Israelis claimed they were trying to capture some terrorists and the Palestinians said they were being attacked for no reason. While the truth will probably never be known, and makes no difference, the result to the Mansour family was the same; for Fatima, two people she had loved dearly were dead and Jamil and Samira had lost a father.

When that occurred, she vowed that she would remove her children from the war zone and into a school in England or the United States. Two people she had loved dearly were dead and Jamil and Samira had lost a father. This reality fueled Jamil's intense views on the subject.

Thankful for the day's events to take over her mind, Fatima watched the clock all afternoon waiting and waiting for 3pm to arrive. The more she watched, the slower it seemed to go. Finally, she had the oven turned off, the trays washed and all the ingredients weighed out for the next day's baking. As she crossed the parking lot to her 1988 red Toyota she kept trying to think of what Jamil may have forgotten. Fortunately, Lansing was only about an hour and a half away and an easy ride on I-96. She smiled, if he forgot something important it would give her and Samira a good excuse to go visit him.

By the time she arrived home, Jamil had his things packed and ready to go. They loaded the car and headed off. Even though it was a little out of the way, they stopped at Shawarma King in Warren for a quick dinner. Eating out was rare, but this was a special day. After dinner, neither said much: he was thinking of the fun to be had back with the friends he had made during the past year, parties and football weekends; she was thinking of how lonely it would be with him no longer at home. Having moved students in and out for over a century, Michigan State was well organized and with a little help from their staff, Jamil was settled in after about three hours. Fatima looked into her son's eyes. He knew she was about to cry.

"Mom, come on, we'll see each other regularly. You're less than two hours away." She nodded and he gave her a big hug. He appreciated all that she had sacrificed so he could attend college and have a good future.

Once in his room, Jamil took out his most valuable possession—a new Apple computer for which his mother had worked extra hours to buy. Even though she was driving away, her warm glow still covered him. He wondered what he could do to show her how much he appreciated her. He put that unanswered question on the shelf along with his used text books.

The gloom of leaving her son was reflected in the mood of the weather slowly turning from clouds to rain. Her tears were reflected in the rain drops slowly spattering on her windshield as she pulled onto the highway. It was a lonely drive home but Fatima knew she needed to go to bed promptly so she could again rise at 3:30am for another day's work. However, as was the case this morning, the lengthy ride gave her more time to think and feel.

When she let her mind drift back to the fateful day 14 years ago when her husband went off to work for the last time, the unexpected shock of learning that her husband was killed just an hour after his strong arms gave her a good-bye hug only re-enforced the fragile nature of life itself. In an hour's time, a warm loving hug could be eternally terminated by a bullet whose job it was to do death efficiently. She was only 28 at the time.

She worried about her son and his almost militant views. While Samira had joined OneVoice, a group of Israelis and Palestinians trying to stop the violence and create two states living in peace, Jamil, in his first year at MSU, joined the Muslim Student Association. Whenever Jamil brought home religious or political views that seemed extreme to Fatima, she pointed out why she believed those views to be extreme. Her logic usually prevailed.

Both mother and daughter believed if these groups could live in peace here in the Detroit area, they should be able to exist peacefully elsewhere. Muslims did their jobs, went to school, had their family lives and practiced Islam. Jews did their jobs, went to school, had their family lives and practiced Judaism. Neither interfered with the other.

As Fatima pulled in the driveway, she was surprised to find the lights out. Too early for Samira to have gone to bed; too late for her not to be at home. Upon entering out of the dark something jumped out at her; Charlie. Fatima quickly verified her initial reaction that Samira was not at home, and a mother's easily tripped worry trigger was set off.

She tried Samira's cell phone; no answer. She called Samira's best friend; she had not heard from her. She called other friends, no information. She called Jamil, he had not heard from her nor knew of any plans she might have had.

Fatima was about to panic and call the police as she finished talking to Jamil when she noticed a Post-it note on the refrigerator which read, "MEC needed me so I went."

Given the hour, Fatima went to bed. As she drifted off into what became another restless sleep, she could not remove her son's hug from her mind - it felt exactly like her husband's last hug.

שתים

A YOUNG MAN'S START

"How can you sit and watch all those detective shows?" Sarah Goodman asked her son for the hundredth time. Jacob's answer for the hundredth time was the same, "Mom, they're not just detective shows, they're criminal investigation shows."

His sister Jenny added, "But every week you DVR 'CSI', 'Bones', '911', and about a thousand others."

"Yeah, and this summer I read this awesome book Hidden Evidence: *50 True Crimes and How Forensic Science Helped Solve Them.* You guys, it's not that I'm just obsessed. It's that someday I'm going to use all the stuff I know about this kind of technology to prevent crimes and terrorist activity."

"Ok, Sherlock Holmes, I have to go to sleep because someone in this family has to earn a living so you two can continue your education," Sarah interjected.

She had become used to going to bed at 9pm so she could drag herself out of bed at 4am. Her children were very thankful for what she had done for them and kept it quiet so she could obtain her much needed rest. When the alarm went off Sarah sometimes would snooze a few minutes until the alarm jolted her out of bed again. 4am was much too early.

Because she was willing to work the early shift, Sarah had worked her way to an excellent job, managing the kitchen for Universal Studios. Since she started early, she finished early and slid back home before the rush hour traffic. Unfortunately her job was not near her home in Reseda.

Sarah's job was her lifeline to the world. It paid the mortgage on their small home, put food on the table, and was helping Jacob through college. Her reward was that her two children had never been in trouble in school, received top grades and attended Sabbath services at Temple Ahavat Shalom with her.

On this day after work she would drive Jacob to UCSD to begin his second year. She was pleased that as President of Hillel, Jacob had initiated contact with One Voice, a group of Israelis and Palestinians trying to stop the violence in the Middle East and create two states living side by side in peace.

Sarah thought Jacob's strong Israeli views developed because his father and grandfather, were both killed in the same tragic incident. Both worked in the same medical unit which made rounds of the outlying kibbutzim. Their medical trucks were on the way to Ashdot Ya'akov Ihud, a kibbutz in northern Israel near the Golan Heights, and were mistaken for an army convoy by the Palestinians and ambushed. Both were killed by the initial gun fire. That very day she made up her mind, as soon as practical she would leave Israel and move to a safer place like the United States. She felt very sorrowful to leave a country she loved dearly but the safety of her family came first. While she could not stop continuous on-again off-again warfare, she could at least extricate her children from it.

UCSD was about three hours each way. So it would be a very long day for her. Besides the natural beauty of California, another reason Sarah had settled there was that she knew how relatively cheap college tuition was compared to other states.

Sarah hopped in the shower and was out quickly. That was her primary way to wake up in the morning. Second, was the strong coffee she made at work. Not only did the workers need and want it, it kept her going also. However, this day before she left for work she left Jacob a note that he needed to be all packed and ready to go when she returned so she they could leave for campus on time and she could return to Reseda in time to sleep a little before another day at work.

Sarah did not need to leave any notes for her daughter, who was a senior at John R. Wooden High School in Reseda. Even though Jacob was 19 and Jenny only 17, Jenny was the one who kept the house running when Sarah was working.

There was plenty to keep her busy at work so the time seemed to race by. When 4pm arrived she hopped into her 1988 blue Chevy Nova and headed home to find Jacob with his things packed and ready to go.

Even though she had to go past UCSD and then east down I-8, she did so because D. Z. Akins was a very special deli, and she wanted to celebrate her son's return to college.

Jacob had mixed feelings about starting UCSD again. It would be fun to be back with his friends but he would miss both his mother and Jenny. It did not take him long to unload the car which was packed full. When it was time for Sarah to leave, Jacob said, "Mom. Thanks for everything" and he gave her a big hug. He could see a few tears in her eyes. He knew it was because of all she had done for him for nineteen years. In addition, each day when her husband had left for work, he gave a hug. Later in one such day, he was killed.

As Jacob unpacked he reflected on how lucky he was to be in San Diego, a great city close enough that he could easily take a train home for the weekend. Occasionally, Sarah and Jenny would drive down and visit him.

When he had most of his possessions in place, he found a book that the rabbi at Hillel had lent him at the beginning of summer. He quickly grabbed his lap-top and wrote:

>To: Rabbi_Cohen@Hillel.org
>From: JacobCA@gmail.com
>Subject: Book
>Date: 25 September 98
>
>>The book you gave me to read over the summer, *By Way of Deception* by Victor Ostrovsky, was excellent. I had trouble putting it down.
>>
>>I had been giving serious thought to doing a forensic science major because I have taken so many science courses and really like them. The Mossad uses everything including technology to gain intelligence. This book helped me make my decision to work towards a degree in forensic science.
>>
>>Thanks again for giving me the book. I am sorry I have not returned it earlier. As soon as I get back to campus I will bring the book to your office.
>>
>>Jacob

On the long drive home, Sarah's mind wandered to finances, as it often did. Having two kids in college at the same time would be more than she could afford but she did not want Jenny to wait until Jacob finished. She was thankful that there were student loans available and she hoped that Jenny, like Jacob, would be awarded some scholarships based on both academic excellence and need.

When Jacob was at school, Jenny had her mother to herself. She missed her brother, but enjoyed the time she had with her mother. To Jenny, she was a survivor first-class. To come to the United States speaking only Hebrew and Yiddish with no job, two young children and no husband and survive was to be admired.

Sarah wished her husband could be here to see his children. It had been tough as a widow to raise two young children in the Jerusalem area in the early 1980s. Her husband's death watered her seed of hatred for war which fully blossomed shortly thereafter. As a result she did what she had to in order to avoid being caught up in the Middle East fighting. It would be easy to hate the faceless "Palestinians" who killed her husband. But, who should she hate? All Arabs? All Muslims? Just Palestinian-Muslims?

Sarah realized she was tired and should not be daydreaming while driving. As she turned into the driveway she realized that Jenny probably had not gotten the day's mail, so she stopped and picked it up. Instead of the two or three bills and a few pieces of unsolicited ads and credit card offers that seemed to always wander into her mailbox, there were three letters for Jacob.

Abraham's Tears

Three
CHURCH RAFFLE

Pastor Fitzgerald slowly began his sermon. "Each year the St. Paul's Lutheran Church here in Sydney has a different type of fund raiser. Usually it is some type of auction. This year we are going to try something different, we are going to raffle off a two week tour for four to the Holy Land in August of next year. Tickets will be $20 each or seven for $100. Sales will begin next week, one year before the trip and the drawing will be on 1 March 2000. That way you will have plenty of time to purchase tickets for yourselves, as anniversary gifts, as Christmas presents, birthday presents, etc. Those of you in business can purchase and use them as rewards for employees or for honored customers. Remember the ticket donation is tax deductible and 100% goes to our church since the trip has been donated by the tour group.

Abraham's Tears

Vier
NEW BUSINESS

On Monday morning as Hans Bernise entered his lab he noticed that there were already three emails for him to deal with. He wanted to get back to the experiments that he left on Friday and he quickly disposed of the first two. The third was from Albrecht Wolf, the Director of Business Development which informed him that the company had for a number of months been in contact with an Israeli desalination research company. The two companies had concluded that the combination of the Israeli desalination technology merged with German delivery technology was a good marriage and an agreement had been reached. He was to go to Israel and work out the technical details.

Abraham's Tears

خمسة

DECISIONS, DECISIONS

Jamil was somewhat surprised and disappointed when the answers from UCLA, the University of Minnesota, Temple, Penn State and Kentucky all came back negative. Later, when the University of Arizona, Duke, the Pasteur Institute, Yale and Oregon State all came back negative he felt depressed; he was not even on a waiting list anywhere. Out of all of the applications that he'd sent out, he thought he would at least be admitted to one of the schools, and he'd even hoped for a scholarship to help his mother out financially.

There were only a few other colleges that he was waiting to hear from. The week of finals, four envelopes arrived, the last four. When Jamil arrived home after finals, he first gave Fatima a big hug, a big "Hi" to Samira and a smaller "hi" to Charlie. He then headed for the small, round oak table near the front door where the mail was deposited. He quickly grabbed the four envelopes addressed to him. The return addresses were the University of Wisconsin, the University of Illinois, King's College London and the University of Connecticut. He slowly shuffled them not wanting to face further rejection. Fatima and Samira looked on with anticipation, but not knowing what to say.

Jamil said, "I need to change my luck. I'm going to turn them face down, shuffle them and then let you pick one for me to open. Just like a card trick." He held out the four for Fatima to pick one. He picked up the dinner knife the Mansour family used as a letter opener, opened the envelope, slid out the letter and read, "The University of Connecticut regrets to inform you...." Well, no reason to read further. Jamil then picked up the remaining three face down and held them out to Samira. She selected the middle one and handed it back to Jamil. He then opened that one, slid out the letter and read, "The University of Wisconsin is pleased to inform you ...." "YES, YES!" Jamil screamed.

"What else does it say?" asked Fatima.

"The University of Wisconsin is pleased to inform you that we will waive out-of-state tuition and provide a scholarship for in-state tuition. In addition, we will provide $500 a semester to cover the cost of books. However, you will be responsible for your room and board."

"Wow, I can't believe it. We pay my room now and most of my tuition. It will cost us less for me to go to Wisconsin than MSU."

"Isn't it much colder in Madison than in Lansing?" asked Samira.

"Oh, who cares how cold it is! I'll wear layers! Wisconsin's excellent reputation will help me get into grad school. And it's cheaper, which means there's something left when I'm done for you to go to college."

Fatima sat down and a few tears ran down her face. "I hoped for this but it didn't look too good. The other schools don't know what a quality person they are missing out on. How should we celebrate?"

"I want to treat us to dinner at Shawarma King. I have been getting in extra hours at Middle East Carpets. Let's go!"

Fatima smiled at her daughter's generosity. "Shouldn't Jamil open the other two envelopes before we go?" she asked.

"Who cares what they say," said Jamil. "Now I have a great deal for next year." He bit his lip and eyed the unopened envelopes. "But I guess it will only take a minute."

He opened one and read, "The University of Illinois regrets to inform you ...." He then picked up the last envelope.

"King's College London is pleased to acknowledge that you have been awarded a scholarship for tuition, half of your room and board...." Jamil exclaimed, "I can't believe it! This is unreal; all those rejections and now not one, but two scholarships! This is wild."

Fatima broke in, "Keep reading. Keep reading."

"The scholarship is limited to one year. You will be responsible for your transportation to and from King's College London. In addition, you will be assigned a work-study project over the winter break. For your information, another Arab student, Hasan, from Jordan has also been offered a scholarship and hopefully will be attending. Your application indicated that you are fluent in Arabic and we may request your assistance in helping Hasan if he has trouble with some English. If so, you will be paid for helping him at our usual tutor hourly rate. Because others have applied for and are interested in obtaining this scholarship, in the event you decide not to accept it, please acknowledge your acceptance of it by signing below and returning this letter to us before March 15th."

Fatima quickly added, "That is about as good as the Wisconsin one, but you wouldn't be home until summer would you?"

"No, I guess I wouldn't. Jamil stared at his family. "I'm stunned. Nothing all fall and now, not one but two! This is crazy."

"Now you have a new problem," said Samira, "deciding which one to accept."

"Best kind of problem to have. Now let's go eat and celebrate!"

שׁשׁ

PLANNING AHEAD

The following day after work Sarah sent the following email and engaged in sequential correspondence:

    To: JacobCA@gmail.com
    From: Sarah.GoodmanCA@yahoo.com
    Subject: Mail
    Date: 10 September 98

        You received three fairly large envelopes yesterday. The return addresses are Arcadia University, Penn State and Nebraska Wesleyan University. Do you want me to leave them for you to open or do you want me to open them and read them to you? What are these about?

        I miss you already. How did your meeting go about the OneVoice program?

        Love, Mom

    To: Sarah.GoodmanCA@yahoo.com
    From: JacobCA@gmail.com
    Subject: Re: Mail
    Date: 11 September 98

Mom, Sorry I forgot to tell you that I was researching schools that offer degrees in forensic science. It's a bunch of schools sending me info.

No need to open them, just leave them for me. It's nothing urgent, just scholarship applications and stuff.

Next year Jenny will also be in college. I don't see how we can afford to cover both of us even if we get scholarships. I'm hoping for some kind of forensic science scholarship money, work study, grants or tuition waivers for next year. And if I can find a job doing forensic science work for just one year, I get that experience, plus one year's pay. I really don't want another In-N-Out type job next summer.

The OneVoice meeting was great. Miss you guys.

Love, Jacob

Later, other emails:

To: JacobCA@gmail.com
From: Sarah.GoodmanCA@yahoo.com
Subject: Mail
Date: 23 September 98

The past week two more letters for you arrived. These are from Boston University and Florida University.

Will you make it home for Rosh Hashanah?

Love, Mom

To: Sarah.GoodmanCA@yahoo.com
From: JacobCA@gmail.com
Subject: Re: Mail
Date: 24 September 98

Yes, I will be home for RH, and will go through my mail then.

Love, Jacob

School was going well for Jacob and his position as president of Hillel required only a few hours a week of his time. He had a part-time job working Sundays at an In-N-Out Burger. In the few hours of his spare time he continued searching for opportunities in forensic science which would put less of a financial burden on his mother.

> To: JacobCA@gmail.com
> From: Sarah.GoodmanCA@yahoo.com
> Subject: Mail
> Date: 26 October 98
>
>> You are very popular, more mail this week. These are from Albany State University and the Forensic Science Institute (University of Central Oklahoma).
>>
>> I am looking forward to having you home at Thanksgiving.
>>
>> Love, Mom
>
> To: Sarah.GoodmanCA@yahoo.com
> From: JacobCA@gmail.com
> Subject: Re: Mail
> Date: 27 October 98
>
>> It'll be good to be home and see you guys.
>>
>> Love, Jacob

Then after meeting with his advisor to schedule courses for the second semester, Jacob began this chain of emails:

> To: Rabbi_Cohen@Hillel.org
> From: JacobCA@gmail.com
> Subject: Can We Meet?
> Date: 12 December 98

> I just completed my meeting with my advisor and he gave me some ideas that I would like to discuss with you.
>
> Happy Chanukah.
>
> Jacob

To:JacobCA@gmail.com
From: Rabbi_Cohen@Hillel.org
Subject: Re: Can We Meet?
Date: 13 December 98

> Of course. However, the semester is almost over and finals begin in just two days. I have to complete a number of things before the end of the calendar year. How about at the beginning of the second semester. Would January 14th at 3:30 work for you?
>
> Happy Chanukah to you.
>
> Rabbi Cohen

To: Rabbi_Cohen@Hillel.org
From: JacobCA@gmail.com
Subject: Re: Can We Meet?
Date: 14 December 98

> Yes that's fine, see you then.
>
> Jacob

Jacob enjoyed being home for the winter break. There was Chanukah and the latkes that went with the holiday. He worked some at the In-N-Out Burger off I-5. Because many of the Christian workers did not want to work around Christmas and New Year's, he was able to take a few extra shifts.

New Year's came, then second semester and January 14th. At his meeting with Rabbi Cohen he mentioned that he had discussed the selection of a forensic science major with his advisor. The advisor noted from his record that he was fluent in Hebrew.

The rabbi asked, "And what did he recommend?"

"A couple of things. He said that lots of students in my financial situation look to the Army as well as scholarships. And that ROTC scholarships are full-tuition and based on a student's merit. Since I've been on the Dean's High Honor Roll, I should have a good chance. He also said there are separate allowances for books and fees as well as stipends that are worth up to $5,000 annually. If I got into the Army, when I graduated, I'd be an officer."

Rabbi Cohen sat back and nodded. "That program would permit you to obtain your graduate degree on a fellowship, relieving your mother of the burden of tuition," he said.

Jacob nodded. "And my advisor thought that because I'm fluent in Hebrew, and given the Middle East situation, I should have an excellent chance with Army Intelligence."

"But Jacob," said the rabbi, "do you truly have an interest in the military?"

"Honestly, I really don't. But after talking to my advisor, I'm really considering it."

"It does offer experience in forensic science as well as solve your financial problems. That gives me an idea. You enjoyed the book *By Way of Deception* about the Mossad, which relies very heavily on technology and forensic science to do their work. But, they do not offer scholarships and it is very difficult to be accepted into the Mossad. However, because you were born in Israel, you are eligible for the Israeli Defense Forces [IDF] which would give you the same experience as the United States Army, with a shorter commitment. In addition, if you do well it would be a good stepping stone to move to the Mossad, if you were interested. If you did your two years with the IDF, you would have excellent experience and you would be able to save money to cover your undergraduate education. Then you could either go to graduate school or you would have a good chance to obtain a position with the Mossad."

"Wow."

"So much to think about, I know, Jacob. All good things. Instead of the U.S. Army, it may be the Israeli Army. Most students don't have the choice; you do. And if you decide to go that route, I would be pleased to help you."

"I will definitely think about it. Thank you so much. I will let you know what I decide."

Choices, choices. Jacob could continue at UCSD for two more years. He could seek scholarships at other schools and if they offered more money, he could transfer and go there to obtain his BS degree. He could go to the Army ROTC and have them pay his undergraduate and graduate training and obtain some valuable experience. Or, with Rabbi Cohen's help, he could try the IDF, gain experience and save his pay to be able cover his expenses when he resumed his education. Jacob's head was spinning.

> To: Sarah.GoodmanCA@yahoo.com
> From: JacobCA@gmail.com
> Subject: Re: More Mail
> Date: 2 February 98
>
>> Mom, a while back I filled out a ton of scholarship applications to complete my undergraduate degree. There were also some applications for summer jobs

and stuff. Sorry if your mailbox looks like the post office.

I am so busy this semester with school and the details of OneVoice. I hope to be home for spring break and will take care of the mail then.

Love, Jacob

To: JacobCA@gmail.com
From: Sarah.GoodmanCA@yahoo.com
Subject: Re: More Mail
Date: 8 March 98

You were not kidding about more mail. But what is this from the Army, IDF and Air Force? I was not aware you had an interest there. You know how I feel about the military.

Love, Mom

To: Sarah.GoodmanCA@yahoo.com
From: JacobCA@gmail.com
Subject: Re: More Mail
Date: 11 March 98

Mom, the Army, Air Force and IDF all use forensic science to investigate crimes and to prevent future ones. I just want to see what they offer.

I will be home in a week to open the mail and see if I have some better deals for next year.

Love, Jacob

While many UCSD students headed to Mexico, Arizona and Texas to have a fun time during spring break, Jacob headed home, eager to review all of the material awaiting him. He felt relaxed because at worst, if none of the information interested him or wasn't a better deal than he now had, he could always stay at UCSD and finish his BS degree as he originally planned.

"Hey Sherlock," said Jenny, "are you interested in the IDF because of forensic science or do you think it's the answer to Israel's Middle East problems? I don't think military force will bring us closer to peace. A two-state solution is the only way for Jews and Arabs to coexist over there."

"But the Palestinians aren't interested in peace. They're interested in wiping Israel off the map. They've rejected every attempt at peace since 1948." Jacob responded. Though these arguments never seemed to resolve, Jacob missed these volleyball matches with his younger sister and found himself impressed with her ability to keep always return the ball to his court.

"I think most Palestinians are peaceful and do want peace," she said. "They have no way to stop Hamas or Hezbollah. And did you know that if they speak out against the terrorists, they are considered traitors and punished? It doesn't help that the Israeli military treats them like prisoners."

"Yeah, and Israel wouldn't treat them like prisoners if they weren't constantly trying to blow up buses. As long as there are Palestinians, there will be terrorism. Sorry, but it's true."

"But how can we punish an entire population for the crimes of just a few people?"

"But you can't deny that those few people make a huge impact. How can you not punish terrorists?"

"But...the Palestinian Authority has already said they like the idea of a two-state solution except

Israel has all these restrictions on trade and they haven't given them a real chance."

"We gave them Gaza and look what happened. They still shoot the same number of rockets into Israel."

"Okay Jacob, let's just say we agree to disagree. You process your applications. I have to go to soccer."

Each night when Sarah came home, she inquired about what Jacob had learned from the letters he had opened and read that day. He kept telling her he'd work through all of them, do the calculations, and then discuss with her and Jenny.

Finally, he was done. He said that the scholarships had come back in one of three categories. One was a polite, "We are sorry we cannot offer you any financial assistance." The second was a group which offered a variety of tuition waivers, partial tuition scholarships, and help with living expense and/or books. But most of these came from private schools or schools with out-of-state tuition. Even if they offered substantially more money than he was receiving now, because the out-of-state or private tuition was so high, it would cost him more to use the financial aid than to stay at UCSD. The last group, Boston University, the Forensic Science Institute at the University of Central Oklahoma and Penn State, offered to cover almost everything.

Sarah was a little bewildered, "You mean even though the tuition and room and board at Boston U, the Oklahoma place and the University of Pennsylvania are more than UCSD, those places will give you enough so that our out of pocket expense is less than it is now?"

"Yup!"

"And those schools have good programs in what you want?"

"Yup! Especially the University of Pennsylvania."

Jenny asked, "What about the Army and the IDF?"

"Well, if I go either of those routes, experience and money are excellent. With the Army, I will just owe them a couple of years when I finish school. With the IDF I have to drop school probably for two years."

"Then it's great you have the offers from Boston, Oklahoma and Pennsylvania. Which one do you think you will choose?"

"I don't know. I have to look into each school some more before I make a decision."

Seven
SELLING TICKETS

On the ride home from church Pat Doerr began the conversation, "We usually donate $500 to the church. That amount would purchase 35 tickets. We can use them as Pastor Fitzgerald suggested. While the Pastor suggested them as birthday or Christmas gifts, I doubt that either of our kids would be pleased to receive a raffle ticket as a gift. However, we can use them for our other relatives."

Her husband, John, added, "Please remind me to notify my sisters. Even though they are not members of our church, they love these events. Ella has plenty of available funds of not only her own funds but she most likely will buy some for her insurance agency."

"I agree."

Abraham's Tears

Acht
A LETTER

Water Engineering Corporation of Berlin
Budapester Struffe 45
10787 Berlin

26 May 2000

Dear Dr. Aaron Goldberg
Ashkelon Desalination
Ashkelon, Israel

Dear Dr. Goldberg:

Albrecht Wolf informed me that our companies have finalized the agreement we were negotiating. He suggested that to move forward I should make arrangements to meet with you to work out the scientific details. I am available to come to Israel the last two weeks in June and the middle two weeks of July.

Respectfully,

Hans Bernise, PhD
VP of R&D

Abraham's Tears

تسعة

A LONG WAY FROM HOME

As British Airways flight BA 5476 approached the Heathrow airport, Jamil looked out the window at the Tower of London. Once on the ground he went through Immigration and Customs and then quickly enjoyed the newness of the Euro and the British accent. He was met by a student ambassador, Stuart, from King's College.

It was agreed that Jamil would secure his bags, then meet Stuart across the bus lane at the sign which advertised tours to Churchill's underground wartime headquarters. Crossing the bus lane after looking left, Jamil's relaxed fascination with London came to a halt when a loud horn and screeching brakes startled him. This was a lesson he realized he must learn fast; in the United Kingdom they drive on the "wrong side" of the road.

At the university he met his roommate, Dave Anderson from Norway, and Hasan. Jamil and Hasan quickly became friends speaking mostly Arabic. Dave was quiet but was always ready to play or watch a soccer match. Having learned that Jamil was born in Palestine, Dave became very interested in Jamil's perspective of the Middle East. One evening after dinner Dave said, "I'm curious what you think is going to happen over there in the next few years."

"I don't think much will happen in the next few years. Israel has the military strength to overrun Palestine, but I don't think they will. Everyone would hate them if they did and it would unite the Arab and Muslim countries against Israel. The Palestinians don't have the ability to take the land that is ours. So the stalemate will continue until hopefully the Arab and Muslim nations can convince the West not to back Israel. If that does not happen, the stalemate will continue."

Jamil continued, "The Arab and Muslim countries would like to settle the matter through peaceful negotiations; personally I would like to see that. However, the Israelis are not reasonable and will not return to us the areas of land that are ours, which they have taken, including our religious places in Jerusalem so it can be out capital. They will not agree to the return of Arabs to their homes and land that was taken from them.

In the days that followed, Jamil and Hasan took tours of Big Ben, Parliament, Buckingham Palace, and more. They even went to see Wimbledon. Dave brought them to a soccer match and they found that this was the activity they both liked most. Jamil had been to college football games, and Hasan to regional soccer matches but they were both amazed as to how the British crowds really got into it.

They also visited various Arab groups which they felt more at home with than they expected. Even though they were from different parts of the world, since they spoke Arabic, they were accepted as brothers.

One day they each received a letter from Mohammad Saeed, the director of the University's Student Muslim Brotherhood, inviting them to a meeting at the Birmingham Central Mosque. Both had heard of the Muslim Brotherhood and were impressed that they were active in knowing where fellow Arabs were.

When school began, both Jamil and Hasan felt grateful for the opportunity to attend. They enrolled in the same courses so they could study together: Eng 155 (English History 1800s), Bio 127 (advanced biology) and Poli Sci 141 (Middle East). Hasan took Bus 111 (Introduction to Accounting) because of his dad's business. Jamil took Math 101 (beginning calculus) because he had not taken a college math course and he needed at least one. Jamil liked Bio and Poli Sci best; Hasan liked Poli Sci and Business.

Jamil liked the hands-on biology experiments better than calculus because calculating the integral of a function from zero to infinity seemed like an impractical theological concept. In particular, he was fascinated when they began genetics. He learned that by using just a few drops of blood, his professor could most likely could distinguish each of the 11 students in his class from one another.

"Down here on the table are 11 serological tubes for blood samples," said Professor Whitehead. "Each is labeled with my name, and a letter from A through K. If you want to participate, take one tube over to Student Medical Services and they will draw less than a teaspoonful of your blood and send it to me for analysis not marked with your name, but only with the letter which *you* select without my knowledge. Today is Wednesday and if you go have your blood drawn this week I should have all the samples by Monday. Then I will bring the results to class next Wednesday." When class was over Hasan and Jamil each picked up a tube, letters H and I respectively. They went together and had their blood drawn the next day.

> To: Fatima.Mansour@yahoo.com; Samira@gmail.com
> From: JamilM@gmail.com
> Subject: Hello
> Date: 27 September 99
>
>> I miss you guys. Even though I was hesitant, I'm glad I chose King's College over Wisconsin. There is no way to learn what this is like without coming here. I can't really describe it. Hopefully one day you can come and visit.
>>
>> Rub Charlie behind the ears for me!
>>
>> With love, Jamil

Jamil and Hasan went together to Friday prayers at the Birmingham Central Mosque. Mohammad invited them to a meeting the next day which was to plan for the winter break "pilgrimages to the Middle East." Both declined, Hasan said he was from Jordan and the Middle East is his home. Jamil told Mohammad that as part of his scholarship, he had to stay and work in London. Mohammad informed him that there was a winter break seminar series in London for local Muslims and he would put Jamil's name on the list. The seminar series was four evenings in one week on various issues and was scheduled in the evening for students who worked day shifts.

Both Hasan and Jamil were hoping the meeting of the Arab students would be both social as well as political. Wrong. There was no time for social niceties, the meeting leaders were very serious about updating students on current issues of concern to Arabs throughout the world. A sign-up list was passed around about the free vacation to the Middle East as well as the local seminar series in London. Jamil saw his name on the latter and thought why not.

Jamil was daydreaming about the week being half over and the cute girl in math that usually sat right in front of him, when he and Hasan arrived for their Wednesday Bio class. He had half-forgotten about the professor's plan to identify each student from others in the class by way of the blood test. Professor Whitehead informed them that he had received blood samples from all 11 students in the class and had analyzed them. "You will recall that when you started the semester the Student Medical Services did a blood type and Rh factor test for each of you so you would be able to obtain immediate medical attention should you ever need emergency care. Would all of you please stand up? As I am able to identify each of you to the exclusion of the others, you may sit down. First, I will separate you into two groups based on sex; XX chromosomes create females and XY chromosomes produce males. We have four XX or females in the group, they are students A, G, J and K. One of the four of you, student A, has blood type AB. Whoever that is, please sit down." One female student sat down. "Further, only one of you has type O blood, student K you may sit down. The other two of you, G and J, are both type B and Rh+. Student G is a Caucasian and student J is of Indian/Pakistan/Afghanistan ancestry, so I can easily separate the two of you." The last two women students sat down.

"Now for the seven males who carry the Y chromosome. One, student, D, carries blood type B; would you please sit down. Three of you, B, C and E, are all blood type A. One of you, E, is Rh-, while the other two of you are Rh+; would student E please sit down."

Professor Whitehead continued. "As you are aware the Y chromosome does not come in pairs. Every human male has only one copy of that chromosome. Because of this there is no lottery as to which copy to inherit, and also no shuffling between copies by recombination. Hence, there is effectively no randomization of the Y-chromosome haplotype between generations, and a male should largely share the same Y chromosome as his father, and grandfather, and great grandfather, give or take a few mutations. In particular, the Y-DNA for genealogical and popular discussion is sometimes referred to as the 'DNA signature' of a particular male human or of his paternal bloodline. Using the haplotype analysis, I find that student C's male parentage is Caucasian and probably Germanic, whereas student B's male parentage is probably Negroid. Therefore, would the two of you please sit down."

"That leaves three of you left," explained the professor, "F, H and I. All three of you are type O and Rh+, so those blood typings do not help. Using the haplotype analysis, I can separate the three of you as follows, student F is of Caucasian descent. That leaves H and I, who can be separated because H is of Middle East probably Arab descent whereas I is, ... is, ..., I will use the term hybrid but I want you to understand it is not used in a derogatory sense in any way but only as a means of describing the situation. The data indicates that individual I is a hybrid of Middle East and Caucasian descent."

"Now we will move on to molecular genetics and gene transfer ...."

Jamil interjected, "Excuse me professor ... professor ..."

"I am sorry, do you have a question before we move on?" asked Professor Whitehead.

"Professor, I am student 'I.' It was your opinion that I was of hybrid ancestry," replied Jamil.

"It is not just my opinion, it is what the genetic evidence shows," responded the professor.

"But it is wrong. Both my parents were Arabs of Middle East descent. I was born in Palestine, I speak Arabic, I am of the Islamic faith," came the quick response. "My father grew up near Jordan and lived his entire life in West Bank area. I saw my dad before he was shot by the Israelis when I was five. He was an Arab, certainly not European in appearance in any way. My mother was also born in Palestine and the only way to describe her is Arab."

Jamil's cheeks grew hot as the details of his past poured out, but he could not stop himself. The calculations must have been flawed in some way.

Professor Whitehead countered. "Anyone can learn to speak a language and many people around the world belong to Islam, so that means little. I can only report what the blood analysis shows. It is possible that something contaminated the testing material. It is also possible, but unlikely, that I made a mistake. But in doing this for over a decade, I don't ever recall an error of this type. The easy way for me to confirm or invalidate this analysis is first, have you give another blood sample to rule out switching of the samples or contamination and second, for you to obtain a blood sample from your mother or sibling."

"Would my mother be able to have a sample drawn in the States and sent here?" Jamil asked.

"Blood banks are in the business of shipping blood. If she will donate a pint of blood, most blood banks will send a sample to a designated location without charge. In addition, since they are in the business of shipping blood, they have all the necessary licenses and permits to ship blood even to other countries. So...."

"But she's really busy with her job and I don't know that she'd have time to find a blood bank and all."

"Do you have any uncles or aunts?"

"My mother had a sister. Her sister and husband were killed at the same time my dad was killed."

Jamil was aware that the others in the class were becoming more and more drawn into his story and his face still felt flushed, however he had to know what all of this meant.

"Do you have any brothers and/or sisters?" asked the professor.

"I have one sister who lives in the States."

"Excellent, most college medical facilities will help each other. If she would go to the equivalent of our Student Medical Services and ask ...."

"Excuse me Professor, but my sister is a senior in high school."

"That shouldn't be a problem. If she can go to a blood bank and give a pint of blood, they will send a sample to me. There will be no cost to her and she will have done a good deed for both you and the recipient! You have my address, correct?"

"Correct."

"Then I can compare your blood and your sister's. This is an excellent real world application of genetics for the class to experience."

> To: SamiraM@gmial.com
> From: JamilM@gmail.com
> Subject: Hi
> Date: 4 October 99
>
> How goes it back in the States? How is school? How is Mom doing? I am getting to know Hasan and Stuart. I relate to Hasan better and we are having a good time. Thankfully, he is also a Shiite, I was concerned that he might be a Sunni, which would be awful. School is hard. The Arab meetings are much more intense here than at MSU. I was shocked and most uncomfortable when some discussed becoming suicide bombers.
>
> In biology we are doing a genetic family tree. I know this might sound weird, but it would really help if I could obtain a sample of your blood. If you would donate a pint at the local blood bank they would then ship a sample, free of charge, to my professor. I know it seems strange but I really need you to do it. I will explain more later. They should send the sample to Dr. John Whitehead, Professor of Cell Biology, King's College London, Strand, London WC2R 2LS, England, United Kingdom. If they need the phone number it's 44 (0)20 7836 5454.
>
> Do you think you could find a cheap student flight and come visit over Spring Break? I think you would really enjoy London and you could meet Hasan and Stuart!
>
> The biggest problem that the three of us have is when we cross the street we keep forgetting to look right and not left!
>
> Love, Jamil

When Jamil was in Michigan he did not realize that the countries of Europe were the size of various states in the United States. Because European countries were so small it was quite easy to travel in Europe. He further learned that a United States passport is good virtually in any country he wanted to go to; he did not need visas. It gave him ideas for spring break. He thought he would like to see France or Germany.

> To: JamilM@gmail.com
> From: SamiraM@gmial.com
> Subject: Blood!
> Date: 6 October 99
>
>> I would love to come and see London, but I can't earn enough. What little I can make during school I want to give to Mom.
>>
>> Totally weird that they need blood for a family tree. But I went yesterday and gave a pint. They said they would send it out that day. You owe me, big bro.
>>
>> Love, Samira

עשר

A DIFFERENT PATH

As the plane was about to land, Jacob kept thinking.... I hope I made the right decision, I hope I made the right decision. Jacob looked out the plane's window as it began its descent asking himself, will I recognize anything? He didn't.

Upon landing at Ben Gurion International Airport near Tel Aviv, he knew it would be slow going through Immigration and then Customs. He had landed at 13:40 but did not have to be ready to be picked up by the bus until 16:00 so this time was not a concern. However, as he moved towards Immigration, there was a soldier holding a sign "Jacob Goodman." Jacob went over and introduced himself, "שלום אני יעקב" [Shalom, I am Jacob] "Good, I am Ari. Come with me, the IDF has a special immigration section, so it goes faster and smoother."

After completing his Immigration screening and a Customs review, Jacob followed Ari to a lounge area. "Jacob, I have to go and fetch two other new recruits. You can stay here and read, sleep, watch TV or use the Internet. Here is a stack of paperwork you will have to complete by tomorrow evening. If you want to begin now, it will save you time tomorrow and make processing easier. The first week is paper work, physicals and orientation; paperwork tomorrow, physical on Tuesday and orientation Wednesday through the Sabbath. The next four weeks are basic training that all recruits must take. After that, you select an area in which to specialize. Different areas of specialization take different lengths of time."

> To: Sarah.Goodman@yahoo.com; JennyCA@gmail.com
> From: JacobCA@gmail.com
> Subject: Hello
> Date: 26 September 99
>
> > I just landed, all is fine.
> >
> > Love, Jacob

Since Jacob knew he had to complete the paperwork in any event, he thought he might as well begin. He was amazed at the detail of the questions but slowly went through answering them. Many were the same as those in his application. He thought the IDF probably did that to see if you gave the same answer both times.

Jacob spent about seven hours on Monday completing his paperwork and on Tuesday spent the entire day taking his medical exam. Following his medical exam Jacob wrote:

> To: Sarah.Goodman@yahoo.com
>   JennyCA@gmail.com
> From: JacobCA@gmail.com
> Subject: Thoroughness
> Date: 28 September 99
>
> > I just completed my physical, it took all day. I have never heard of anything so complete. They examined

areas I never knew I owned. In addition I had to give samples of blood, urine and hair to be analyzed.

Things are great, this place is neat!

I miss you guys!

Love, Jacob

Jacob was surprised as to how much general type material was covered in orientation. He learned about the history about the area, interaction of Israeli governmental agencies, political and ethnic issues of the Arabs, as well as religious issues of both Christians and Muslims. He also learned about the intra-Muslim religious issues of the Sunnis and Shiites and the geopolitical issues of Jordan, Lebanon, Iraq, Iran, and Pakistan. On Friday they were to finish up at 14:00 and then prepare for the Sabbath. The following Monday basic training started. At 14:00 when the new recruits were being instructed about when and where to report on Monday as they were being discharged, the leader asked, "Is Jacob Goodman present?"

"Yes sir. Right here."

"Please report to the medical office at 14:10. The rest of you are dismissed."

Jacob was surprised that, out of the forty or so new recruits, he was the only one asked to report to the medical office. However, it did not concern him and he walked over to the office and introduced himself.

"Mr. Goodman, thanks for coming. Please go down the hall and to the second office on the right and introduce yourself."

Jacob did as requested. "Shalom, I am Jacob Goodman."

"Thanks for coming. I am Dr. Feinberg. Please sit down. I have a few more questions that I need to ask you. Some may be repetitive, but please bear with us."

"What is your birth date?"

"June 17, 1980."

"What was the name of the hospital where you were born?"

"I wasn't born in a hospital. I was born at home. What is all this about? I gave all this simple information in my application and in the questionnaire I filled out here."

"I will explain in a few minutes, but first I need to go through some of these questions to make sure we have them correct. Who was the doctor that delivered you?"

"There was no doctor, I was told by my mother, a midwife delivered me."

"What is your mother's complete name?"

"Sarah B. Goodman."

"What does the B. stand for?"

"Braufman."

"What was your dad's complete name?"

"David Irving Goodman."

"Do you know who filled out your birth certificate?"

"No, I have no idea who did."

"You said your dad was working in a medical unit 14 years ago when he was killed by a Palestinian ambush."

"Correct."

"Do you know where he is buried?"

"Yes, somewhere here in Israel. But I don't have the name of the cemetery. My mother, sister and I left Israel when I was five and I have not been back until now. But I am sure my mother would know the name if you want me to obtain it."

"No, that won't be necessary. We have the name."

"What is all this about?"

"Let me explain. You appear to be answering truthfully and most all your answers check out fine. However, we can not find your birth certificate. We have your sister's, but not yours. However, you were born in 1980 which was before we began keeping birth certificates electronically by computer. Further, at that time often no birth certificate was filed when a child was born at home especially when no physician was present. No problem, we just wanted to check to make sure we had it correct. Shalom, enjoy the Sabbath."

> To: JennyCAmail.com
> From: JacobCA@gmail.com
> Subject: Hello
> Date: 1 October 99
>
>> Hi. I am glad I made the decision to come here. You may want to look into some of the scholarships that I found especially the one at the University of Michigan. It is an outstanding school and they accept a large number of "foreign students."

How is your soccer team doing? When I left they were in second place.

Love, Jacob

To: JacobCA@gmail.com
From: JennyCAmail.com
Subject: Re: Hello
Date: 3 October 99

Good to hear from you. I'm glad you are pleased with your decision. I will take advantage of your running off to apply for some of the scholarships that you didn't take.

Still second place in our conference, but ranked 10th in the state!

I am very tired. I think it is a combination of school, soccer and working at In-N-Out Burger. There is a redhead there, Lucy, that seems disappointed that you left!

Hope you are enjoying Israel. Keep me updated on your training.

Love, Jenny

Eleven
NOTIFYING SISTERS

To: ERS1@gmail.com; ECDodson@gmail.com
From: BigJohn@gmail.com
Subject: Our Church's Raffle
Date: 12 August 99

Sisters:

This year our church's fund raiser is not an auction. It is something better, it is going to be a raffle, the prize is a two week tour for four to the Holy Land in August of next year. The tickets are $20 each or seven for $100.

Sales start next week. It is like Chicago politics, vote early and vote often. Here you will want to purchase early before the winning ticket is sold and often because the more you purchase the better you chances are.

John

Abraham's Tears

Zwölf
MIXING BUSINESS WITH PLEASURE?

To: Ilse33@yahoo.com
From: HBerniseWECB@gmail.com
Subject: Business trip to Israel
Date: 26 May 00

>Wife:
>
>I need to go to Israel for a few days this summer. Since you are a Baha'i and one of the few Baha'i temples is in Israel, I thought you might want to come along. When business is done, we can take a few days for vacation.
>
>me

Abraham's Tears

ثلاثة عشر
IT CAN'T BE

About a week later, on a Friday at the end of class, Professor Whitehead asked Jamil to see him sometime in his office. Jamil wasn't sure what it was about, but thought maybe it had to do with his sister's blood sample. So later that afternoon, Jamil went to Dr. Whitehead's office. Dr. Whitehead began, "I asked you to give another sample of blood so I could recheck and make sure there was no error. You did and I have your second sample here. I also have you sister's blood sample and I have analyzed that. I thought you would want to actually see the results for yourself. Here are the results of the sample you gave about two weeks ago and the second sample. As you can see they are identical; there was no error. Here is student C, whose parents are Caucasian and both are probably of English descent. Here is student J both of whose parents are of Indian/Pakistan/Afghanistan origin. Can you see the difference?"

"Yes."

"OK, now here is student H, your friend Hasan whose parents are Middle Eastern, probably Arab and you can see how the three differ."

"Yes."

"Good, now here is your sister's and here is yours. Can you see how your sister's is very similar to student H but quite different from yours?"

"That can't be right!"

"You are aware from class that a series of polymorphisms which can be looked at together is termed a haplotype. It is so well accepted that haplotypes can be used to track different ethnic groups that a book has been written about it, *Keeping God's House* by David B. Goldstein. In his book Goldstein explains that his group was able to track one specific group of Jews, the Cohanim using halotypes. They termed that haplotype the Cohen Modal Haplotype. Now back to your situation. Here your and your sister's haplotypes differ...."

"There has to be some error. I know who my dad was and who my mother is. I had the same mother and father as does my sister; I saw them. I know where I was born and where I lived until my mother emigrated from Palestine to the United States."

"I understand. Since this screening analysis showed that you and your sister differ, I went back and did the same analysis one would do in a paternity case on both yours and your sister's samples. As you can see, it clearly shows that you and your sister have different parents."

"No, no, no - that can't be right. I remember my dad, a little. He was my mother's husband and our father. We had the same parents. Maybe...maybe, they sent the wrong blood sample."

"The best way to check that is to obtain a sample of your mother's blood to test. I understand the financial problem, but scientifically, that is the only way to know for sure."

It Can't Be

"I... I ..."

"I asked you to come to my office, since I wanted to disclose this to you privately. I thought you might not be aware of this situation. This is none of my business and as far as I am concerned this information goes no farther than the two of us. I am sorry you learned of this situation this way; this has never happened before in any of my classes. My intent was just to show the identification power of science in general and genetics in particular. You probably have learned more than you desired."

Jamil bewilderedly shuffled down the hall thinking, how could this be, there must be an error somewhere. But, but... these genetic tests which can determine paternity are very sensitive and accurate. I don't want to believe the test, but what if it is correct? What are the possibilities? I need to use the scientific logic I have been taught.

Jamil thought to himself, first, I could have been adopted. I know in the States, adoption is a formal process and often kids are adopted from all over the world including Korea and Romania. But in the Middle East in the early 80s, when both parents were, killed which happened all too often in Palestine, relatives and friends just took in kids and "adopted" them, there was no formal adoption process. The professor said Samira and I had different parents, it could be that she too was adopted but from a different family. Mom is the type of person who would take in someone else's kids if the parents were killed or could not take care of the children. Her sister and sister's husband were both killed in the firefight that killed dad. They lived much to the South of where we lived and I don't recall ever meeting them or their child because the on going hostilities and border checkpoints made it very difficult to travel. I don't recall if mom said their

57

child was a boy or girl. That child would have been about my age. But if I was mom's sister's child, no... no, that can't be because if I were mom's sister's child I would test the same as mom, as an Arab and the same as Hasan, and I didn't.

Second, we have been taught about artificial insemination. Artificially inseminated, in Palestine in 1980, right! As much chance as I have of being Prime Minister of Israel or the Chicago Cubs winning the World Series!

The lawyer, Jawad, lived down the block from us. He was European and went to law school in the UK where he met his wife who was from the Middle East. I remember seeing a picture of him, his wife and their son on the wall in his house. Mom said she died of pneumonia. I don't recall ever seeing or playing with the son. After his wife died, could mom have taken in his son? I am sure he could not work as the judge of our area and take care of a child at the same time. If mom took in his child, it would be like the other informal adoptions. I... I would expect mom to take in his son when his wife died and he was unable to take care of the child. That would be mom! That would also explain why we were at his house almost daily. Mom said it was so he could teach us English, that may be true. But it also would have facilitated his seeing his son.

Jamil thought, what will I say to Hasan when I see him? He knows I went to see the professor. Hopefully, he won't remember.

As soon as Jamil left the professor's office, he headed for the library where he sent the following:

> To: Fatima.Mansour@yahoo.com
> From: JamilM@gmail.com
> Subject: Biology
> Date: 12 October 99

How are you? I miss both you and Samira. How is Samira? School is going well.

I am getting to know Hasan and Stuart better; they are quite different. It is a valuable education just to meet and know students from other countries; that is something I could not have done in the States.

Recently in biology class we had a demonstration of genetics. Genes are the things in our cells that are transferred from parents to their children and program who we are. It is like a biological-computer program. It is why most Scandinavians usually have blond hair and are tall and why most all Asians are short and have straight black hair. Parents pass their characteristics on to their children.

From blood samples, our instructor showed us how we can determine the sex of a person, their blood type, Rh factor, etc. For comparison and checking, Samira sent a sample of her blood. There is a problem. The blood samples indicate Samira and I have different parents. I gave a second sample of blood to recheck but I need a blood sample from you. I know you will want to help me. I understand that your health insurance most likely will not cover it. The test is free if you will give a pint of blood at a blood bank.

Please have whoever draws the blood send the sample to Dr. John Whitehead, Professor of Cell Biology, King's College London, Strand, London WC2R 2LS, England, United Kingdom. If they need the phone number it is 44 (0)20 7836 5454.

Love, Jamil

Jamil knew this would shake up his mother, but she was the person that had the answer to the puzzle which involved him. Who were his parents? Was he an Arab? A Muslim? Were he and Samira really brother and sister? Professor Whitehead said they had different parents, did that mean Fatima was not his mother; that couldn't be. Maybe Fatima was not Samira's mother.

"Hi, what did the professor want with you?" asked Hasan when he met up with Jamil.

"Oh, nothing much, I left my name off the last quiz but he recognized my sloppy handwriting," fudged Jamil.

Because London was five hours ahead of the United States Eastern Time zone, Jamil knew that he would not receive an answer until tomorrow at the earliest. He tried reading an Arab pamphlet setting forth the reasons why UN resolution 242 was wrong in not mentioning the Palestinians. According to the UN, the Arabs were not an official party to the conflict and therefore not mentioned. The UN's position was that the Arabs of the West Bank (Judea and Samaria) were Jordanian citizens, just as the Arabs of Gaza were Egyptian citizens. However, his mind kept wondering to who his parents were. Why did Fatima raise him?

Saturday came and went with no response. Well maybe she had a long day at work and spent the remainder of the day with Samira. Maybe she didn't check her email.

Sunday came and went with no response. Well, mom often worked Sundays when others were off and Samira was working and not at home for extra money.

Monday came and went with no response. Jamil used the school workstations to log in and check his email often; nothing. He had trouble concentrating all day. He carried himself through the day minute to minute, not being able to concentrate at all on

It Can't Be

what was said in class. He could not take notes; why attend class?

He left campus and wandered down to his favorite park, Battersea Park. It was his favorite because it was right on the Thames River. He sat down under the shade of a large oak tree. How could this happen to me? One day everything is fine and then the next I learn I am not who I thought I was.

Relax, relax, relax he kept telling himself. What is, is; I can't change it and it will not change. I need to think of the possibilities and then see which are most likely while I am waiting for mom's blood.

If the professor meant both of my parents are different from Samira's parents, then I could have been adopted. But why would mom have adopted me and then had Samira? Ah, maybe she couldn't have children and we are both adopted; the professor couldn't know if either of us was mom's biological child, only that the genetics showed we had different parents. Maybe I am Jawad's son and Samira is mom's sister's child. As Jamil threw a twig in the river and watched it slowly drift down stream meandering from one side of the river to the other. He thought — just like the river of life.

Abraham's Tears

ארבע עשרה

TRAINING EXPANDS

Training continued morning, afternoon and evening daily except for the Sabbath. Jacob was never so glad to see the Sabbath come as it offered the day's rest that God required.

> To: Sarah.GoodmanCA@yahoo.com;
>   JennyCA@gmail.com
> From: JacobCA@gmail.com
> Subject: Moving Forward
> Date: 15 October 99
>
> How are the two of you? I miss both of you. Things are becoming more interesting here as we move further into basic training. I certainly will be glad when this phase is done. I am exhausted.
>
> When we are done with our basic training some of us will have special assignments. We have some input into the process. Because both my interest and many college courses are in forensic science I have a reasonable chance of being placed in something dealing with that.
>
> Let me know what is going on in CA.
>
> Love, Jacob

Jacob went through the daily motions of exercise, learning weapons, history, language, how to intercept communications, hand to hand combat, small arms, how the IDF integrates with the Air Force and special units, etc., but he kept wondering what his special assignment would be. While many of the recruits enjoyed most the weapons training and learning tricks of hand to hand combat, Jacob preferred the less physical and more mental activities such as learning to follow someone without being detected, what to do to make sure you are not being followed, etc.

> To: JacobCA@gmail.com
> From: JennyCA@gmail.com
> Subject: Re: Moving Forward
> Date: 19 October 99
>
> Have you heard anything about your assignment?
>
> I don't know how you kept your schedule of school, Hillel and part-time job. I am exhausted; occasionally I fall asleep in class. I think I will skip soccer practice today and go to bed earlier.
>
> Mom is fine, just busy and she misses you very much.
>
> Love, Jenny

A few days after that Jacob was called to Dr. Feinberg's office. He was told that Dr. Feinberg would like to discuss a possible assignment for him with him.

Dr. Feinberg started slowly informing Jacob that the IDF was aware of his interest in forensic science, Mossad and their activities. Then Dr. Feinberg continued, "When we did the face scans the second day you were here, we noted that you have the facial bone structure more like an Arab than an Israeli.

While it is not common, it is not really rare either. In addition, your hair color and skin are consistent with a number of Arabs. Hence, you could pass for an Arab without much difficulty."

"Me pass for an Arab?" Jacob was surprised.

"Yes. There is a Muslim seminar or conference in London in December on Monday through Thursday evenings sponsored by a local Muslim group and a large conference on Friday morning before Friday prayers sponsored by the very well respected International Interfaith Council on the topic of "Middle East Issues." You should attend that also since you will already be in London. With regard to the Friday program it will be good for you to learn not only how the presenter views the Middle East situation but also the views of the various attendees. The four day program will be attended by a large number of Arab and Asian Muslims. It would be good practice for you to go to the meeting pretending to be an Arab and, at the same time, it would be helpful to us for you to gather data about the participants and what is being discussed. Please give it serious thought and let me know in 72 hours because if you will do it, we need to train you and set up your cover."

A day later Jacob called Dr. Feinberg, and said, "Thank you very much for the opportunity; I would like to try it. However, I don't speak or know any Arabic. If you can work around that, count me in. What's next?"

"Not speaking Arabic is a drawback but not one we can't or haven't dealt with before. The next step is to work out in detail a cover for you. Your cover would explain your being in London, your not speaking Arabic and not knowing much about the Muslim religion, etc. The cover we will use is that your parents had moved to Pocatello, Idaho, when you were very young and they were concerned how the locals who were very conservative would accept an Arab/Muslim family. Therefore, the family quickly became farmers from Thailand and their Arab/Muslim ethnicity/religion evaporated as quickly as water on a hot stone in the summer Pocatello heat. Because instate tuition is cheap, you attended the University of Idaho and then on a student exchange program you are spending a year in a small college in the northern UK. All these are places that it is most unlikely any other Arab/Muslim attending the meeting ever would have been, so no one at the meeting would know you."

Fortunately for Jacob, three years earlier there was another recruit, who now is a Mossad agent, who had the similar facial bone structure and Arab appearance and had done the same thing. He would mentor and help train Jacob. Jacob was informed that there would be extensive and continuous role playing until Jacob became comfortable as Ibrahim Halabi, a senior science major from the University of Idaho, attending the University of Hertfordshire on a student exchange program.

Jacob would be supported by a number of IDF agents in case he ran into any problems. He was to be wired to record conversations where he was close enough to hear even though he did not participate. In addition, his glasses would have a small camera so the IDF could record what Jacob saw. While the IDF/Mossad would like the information he would obtain, he was informed that basically this was a training mission for him to learn how to do this type of work. Jacob thought for a first assignment this was a good step in the learning process.

Practice, role play and rehearse.

Practice, role play and rehearse.

> To: JacobCA@gmail.com
> From: JennyCA@gmail.com
> Subject: ME
> Date: 12 November 99
>
> I have had some positive responses regarding my scholarship applications, particularly from Emory and the University of Michigan. Both seem to be good deals. Winters in Michigan, am I crazy? There are a number of schools like the University of Missouri and Texas Tech where I probably will receive a partial scholarship. I'm glad you gave me the idea of searching for scholarships out of state. I think we are successful because of mom's financial situation combined with our academic accomplishments.
>
> I've been so tired that I missed a bunch of soccer practices and was not eligible for our last game. Mom made an appointment for me to see our family doctor four days from now. I could barely roll out of bed this morning, I must have mono and the Jewish worry gene!
>
> I hope you are given the assignment you want.
>
> Love, Jenny

Practice, role play and rehearse.

Practice, role play and rehearse.

Abraham's Tears

Fifteen
ELIZABETH'S REPLY

To: BigJohn@gmail.com
From: ECDodson@gmail.com
Subject: Re: Our Church's Raffle
Date: 14 August 99

   John:

   Robert and I will purchase seven.

   Eliz

Abraham's Tears

Sechzehn
AN ATHEIST GOING TO ISRAEL?

    To:HBerniseWECB@gmail.com
    From: Ilse33@yahoo.com
    Subject: Re; Business trip to Israel
    Date: 26 May 00

    Hans:

    Of course I will go; glad you scheduled the meeting there rather than here. It should be a lot of fun. I have always wanted to go to see the Baha'i temple there. Friends who have seen it tell me it is outstanding.

    btw – what is your company doing sending an atheist to Israel! You should be the last person traveling to such a religiously significant spot

    wifey

Abraham's Tears

سبعة عشر

EENY, MEENY, MINEY, MOE

Tuesday came and went with no response.

Wednesday came and went with no response.

On Thursday, Jamil was startled to find a response. But just as he was about to click on it to open it, a series of thoughts came to him. Do I really want to see the answer? Do I really want to know? Why can't I just ignore it and go on as if nothing happened? I could, but I should know the truth. If I don't find out now, I will always wonder and ask later. I might as well find out now. Fortunately, I don't think it makes any difference to my continuing in school, my vocation or anything of substantial importance.

> To: JamilM@gmail.com
> From: Fatima.Mansour@yahoo.com
> Subject: Your question
> Date: 19 Oct 99
>
> > I am glad you are doing well. Even though Samira is here, I still miss "the man of the house."
> >
> > I won't send any blood. I will explain everything when you come home in May.

Samira is doing great at school and working to help out. Charlie is misses you also.

Love, Mom

What!?! Explain EVERYTHING? What is "everything?" What's this, "I will explain everything when you come home." That's half a year away!!! I can't wait that long.

>To: Fatima.Mansour@yahoo.com
>From: JamilM@gmail.com
>Subject: Re: Your question
>Date: 19 Oct 99

Mom, I can't wait half a year. Please, please just tell me so I know; you can fully explain the "whys" in May. Regardless of what happened you are my "mom" and always will be; you are the one who brought me up and cared for me. You are the only mother I have ever known and I love you dearly regardless of what the situation is. Please just tell me so I know.

My mind is racing. I could be adopted or Samira and I could both be adopted. In addition, I remember the lawyer Jawad had a son and I don't recall you mentioning what happened to that boy when his mother died. Am I that child? It really does not make any difference to me, I just need to know. Please tell me NOW.

Your son, Love Jamil

No reply for a week. Then,

>To: JamilM@gmail.com
>From: Fatima.Mansour@yahoo.com
>Subject: Re: Your question
>Date: 28 Oct 99

I will explain fully, but only when I can do it in person. Please do not ask again, I will not reply.

I'm glad you made the decision to go to London.

Love, Mom

Jamil was stunned. The professor was right; mom did not deny it. But if she is not my birth mother why won't she tell me who is? Maybe I could convince her that it really does not make any difference to me; just that I want to know. But, she said she would not reply and knowing mom, she will not reply.

The hours and days blurred into each other. One academic course streamed into all the others. Overriding everything was, who were my parents? No matter what Jamil tried to concentrate on — who were my parents? How did Fatima come to raise me?

Monday, Tuesday, Wednesday, Thursday, Friday.

English History, Bio 127, Poli Sci 141, Math 101.

Adopted or the lawyer's son?

Monday, Tuesday, Wednesday, Thursday, Friday.

English History, Bio 127, Poli Sci 141, Math 101.

Adopted or the lawyer's son?

Monday, Tuesday, Wednesday, Thursday, Friday.

English History, Bio 127, Poli Sci 141, Math 101.

Adopted or the lawyer's son?

If one door is closed, try another.

To: SamiraM@gmail.com
From: JamilM@gmail.com
Subject: A big problem, Help!
Date: 4 November 99

I hope everything is going well for you. Any boyfriends?

Your blood sample showed that we have different parents. Our mothers and/or fathers are different. I could not believe it until the professor showed me the results. There is the possibility that the samples were switched or contaminated so I asked mom to send a sample of her blood. She would not send any blood. She said she would explain in May. I can't wait that long to know!

In thinking back I remember the lawyer, Jawad, who taught us English. According to mom, his wife died and they had a son. I recall seeing a picture of the three of them. I don't remember ever seeing or playing with the son, so the "son" could be me. The lawyer could not work as our local judge and take care of a son at the same time. Could mom have taken him in and that could be me? You may remember that mom, you and I spent a lot of time with the lawyer. Mom says it was so you and I would learn English but now I am not so sure that was the only reason.

I could have been adopted. We both could have been adopted.

Mom said she would explain in full when I come home in May. I can't wait that long, I am going crazy not knowing. It is hard to study or do anything; my mind keeps wandering back to the possibilities. I ramble like I am doing now.

Mom won't reply to me. I told her I don't care which of these people may have been my birth parents, mom is "mom" since she has taken good care of me and I love her dearly even though she did not give birth to me. She is the only mom I have known and she always treated me as if I was hers. While mom won't respond to me, maybe she will talk to you since you are there and you also are affected. I am sure you want to know as much as I do whether you are mom's daughter.

You know how to approach mom better than I do. Please try and let me know anything you find out asap.

Even though we are not blood brother-sister, you are my sister. You have always been good to me and I am glad you are my sister.

Your brother, Love Jamil

To: JamilM@gmail.com
From: SamiraM@gmail.com
Subject: Re: A big problem, Help!
Date: 5 November 99

If I did not know you better, I would say you are putting me on. Wow! BIG WOW! Let me think about this for a day or two.

With love, "Your sister"

English History, Bio 127, Poli Sci 141, Math 101.

Adopted or the lawyer's son?

To: JamilM@gmail.com
From: SamiraM@gmail.com
Subject: Information
Date: 8 November 99

I told mom that you had sent me an email indicating that the blood that I sent showed we were not brother and sister. Further, that you wanted a sample of her blood to make sure there were no errors and I could learn if I was her daughter.

She simply said that no blood sample was necessary, that I am her daughter and that you and I did not have the same parents. Then very sternly she told me what she told you — drop the matter now, that she would explain fully in person in May.

I was SHOCKED. But I have to respect her position and I will not ask again. I am sorry for you, I understand your frustration and anxiety.

Even though we are not "brother and sister" I will always regard you as my BIG brother.

Good luck and try to be patient.

"Your sister" Love, Samira

What do you do when all the doors are shut? While Jamil was pondering that question, his cell phone rang, it was Hasan. "Friday night after prayers, a couple of us are going to a movie including that cute girl you have had your eye on. Do you want to join us?"

Adopted or the lawyer's son?

Jamil could not keep his mind off his personal situation and would probably have agreed to run for Miss Israel if asked. "Sure, why not."

שמונה עשרה
TROUBLE

To: JacobCA@gmail.com
From: Sarah.Goodman@yahoo.com
Subject: Jenny
Date: 24 November 99

    How are you doing? I certainly miss you.

    The doctor checked Jenny. The good news is she doesn't have mono. The bad news is they don't know why she is so tired. They will run more tests.

    Let us know about your special assignment if you can.

    Love, Mom

To: Sarah.Goodman@yahoo.com
From: JacobCA@gmail.com
Subject: Re: Jenny
Date: 25 November 99

    The reason I haven't written is that I can not discuss my special assignment.

    Thanks for keeping me updated on Jenny. I sure hope she is OK. Tell her I wish I was there to support her.

    Happy Thanksgiving! I will miss the two of you and your usual excellent turkey dinner.

    Love, Jacob

Finally, game time! Jacob and his team flew to London using assumed identities. The schedule of the Muslim Educational Seminar was:

> Monday—Why Muslims Who Promote Jihad Against the West Misinterpret The Qur'an
> Tuesday—Economic Issues Facing Muslims
> Wednesday—Why Muslims Who Promote Jihad Against the West Correctly Interpret The Qur'an
> Thursday—Self Defense and Military Matters

All programs started at 19:00 and went for about three hours. Jacob was to mingle, listen, say as little as possible and record as much information as he could. The session that they were most interested in was the Wednesday one. By then "Ibrahim" would have had two days experience. It was a totally new experience and a very scary one at that and he was very nervous. He was afraid to shake hands with the other participants because his hands were so sweaty. However, he did his job well, said little, listened a lot and recorded a lot of useful information. The project was successful and Jacob was glad he accepted it. A good start!

Upon returning to Israel with the rest of his team, Jacob resumed the usual training regimen for new recruits. Various recruits were given specialized training, as he had with his mission to London. However, many of the projects were "make work" for training purposes and not real world situations as he was involved in London.

A couple of weeks later he received the following email.

> To: JacobCA@gmail.com
> From: Sarah.Goodman@yahoo.com
> Subject: Jenny
> Date: 14 January 00

HAPPY NEW YEAR!

There is good news and bad news.

The good news is Jenny was offered almost a full scholarship for tuition, room and board at the University of Michigan.

The bad new is the doctors still are not positive what is wrong with Jenny. It may be something called aplastic anemia. I will keep you updated.

Love, Mom

While Jacob was thinking about Jenny's situation he received a call from the leader of the mission to London, Joseph. He informed Jacob that the internal review of the London mission was quite positive, that Jacob had obtained good video and audio and seemed to be well accepted by the Muslims attending the conference. That Jacob attended the London meeting and had been seen by those present would make his acceptance at other meetings easier, as some of the student representatives would recognize him. Further, in the spring there was going to be an Arab summit in Cairo and part of the summit would be a meeting of the student group. Joseph informed Jacob that the IDF would like him to volunteer to do the same information collecting in Cairo because this group was more likely to be militant and the information identifying the leaders and their plans of action would actually be of much more assistance to the IDF. He told Jacob to think on it until the Sabbath, which was four days away. Joseph also told Jacob that if he agreed to go, the IDF would give him a very intense crash course in Arabic to help him jumpstart his undercover career.

Jacob was flattered that he had been asked to participate but was concerned the IDF wanted to use him in undercover work because of his appearance. He really wasn't interested in undercover work; he wanted to use his scientific background. While he was contemplating how to inform Joseph that he appreciated the offer but would rather wait for something that he was more interested in, he received another email from Sarah.

> To: JacobCA@gmail.com
> From: Sarah.Goodman@yahoo.com
> Subject: Jenny
> Date: 18 January 00
>
> Jenny has aplastic anemia. They say it is moderate to severe which can be life threatening. I never heard of it before and I don't believe that you are familiar with it either.
>
> Aplastic anemia is a disease of the blood that in some way stops your stem cells from producing blood. Jenny is tired because she is not producing red blood cells. By not producing platelets her blood will not clot and by not producing white blood cells she is much more susceptible to infection. If it gets worse, it can be life threatening and she will have to be hospitalized.
>
> Blood transfusions are not a cure but do relieve the signs and symptoms by providing the blood cells her body is not making. Right now she needs transfusions to keep her stable.
>
> She may need a bone marrow transplant if the condition gets worse which is what appears to be happening. The doctor told me that since she is young, a bone marrow transplant is likely to not only help, but cure her. With regard to a bone marrow transplant, any donor that matches is acceptable. They don't know if you are a match. You will have to be tested

to see if you are a match. It is just a blood test. I am willing to be tested and donate, but they prefer young donors because their bone marrow is more likely to be successful in a transplant, if they can find a match. Can you apply for a leave of absence and come home, get tested and possibly help Jenny?

Love, Mom

To: Sarah.Goodman@yahoo.com
From: JacobCA@gmail.com
Subject: Re: Jenny
Date: 18 January 00

That's is scary! Jenny was always so healthy playing soccer and all. I will see what I can do about getting a leave of absence.

Do you know what my being a bone marrow donor would involve?

Tell Jenny I am sending her a "BIG HUG and best wishes."

Love, Jacob

To: Joseph@IDF.org
From: JacobCA@gmail.com
Subject: Medical Emergency at home
Date: 19 January 00

I just learned that my sister has aplastic anemia and needs blood transfusions at a minimum and more likely a bone marrow transplant. As her brother, the chances of my bone marrow being an acceptable match is better than a nonsibling's.

Can I apply for a leave of absence? If so, how?

Jacob

To: JacobCA@gmail.com
From: Joseph@IDF.org
cc: Dr.Levine@IDF.org
Subject: Re: Medical Emergency at home
Date: 19 January 00

> Jacob, I am very sorry to hear of your sister's condition. Medical leave decisions are made by Dr. Levine, so I am copying him.
>
> Best of luck to your sister.
>
> Joseph

To: JacobCA@gmail.com
From: Dr.Levine@IDF.org
Subject: Your sister
Date: 20 January 00

> Jacob, aplastic anemia is a very serious condition especially if they think hers may be severe; it could be life threatening. Family and health come first.
>
> If she needs a bone marrow transplant they will replace her diseased bone marrow with healthy bone marrow from a donor who matches and is preferably young. It may offer the only successful treatment option for people with severe aplastic anemia. This is generally the treatment of choice for people who are younger and have a matching sibling donor.
>
> Bone marrow transplantation from a related, matched donor can treat and cure aplastic anemia, without recurrence, in about four out of five cases.
>
> If you are going to be a donor, the diseased bone marrow in your sister is first depleted with radiation or chemotherapy. Healthy bone marrow from you will be extracted through a routine surgical technique. The healthy marrow is injected intravenously into

the bloodstream of the person with aplastic anemia, where it migrates to the bone marrow cavities and may begin generating new blood cells in about three to four weeks. The procedure requires a lengthy hospital stay by her, not you. After the transplant, she will receive drugs to help prevent rejection of the donated marrow.

For the donor it is a simple procedure.

Administratively there are two ways we handle this. Either (1) you will be given a short leave of absence to be a donor and promptly return here or (2) you will be temporarily reassigned to the states and enrolled in a program there that we think benefits our soldiers. I don't make that decision, but I will communicate with you because this is deemed a medical matter.

Dr. Levine

To: Sarah.Goodman@yahoo.com
From: JacobCA@gmail.com
Subject: Jenny
Date: 21 January 00

It looks like I probably will be able to come home and help Jenny. I am just not sure when I will be able to leave and when I will have to return. I will keep you updated. Please keep me updated on her condition.

Love, Jacob

Abraham's Tears

Nineteen
ELLA'S REPLY

To: BigJohn@gmail.com
From: ERS1@gmail.com
Subject: Re: Our Church's Raffle
Date: 18 August 99

John:

You know I am a sucker for these things. I will take $1,000 for the family and $2,000 for the business.

Your crazy sister, Ella

Abraham's Tears

Zwanzig
SCHEDULING

To: HBerniseWECB@gmail.com
From: GoldbergAD@gmail.com
Subject: Our Meeting
Date: 2 June 00

Dr. Bernise:

The people necessary for the meeting will not be here at the times you suggested because of vacations and business travel. The week of August 7th works well for us here.

Aaron

Abraham's Tears

واحد وعشرون
VACATION?

December 20th, winter break, no school, no studying but no vacation. Jamil realized that he would be as busy during the two weeks of the winter break as he was during the school year. But there was no studying and no pressure, the first semester was done.

He owed King's College two weeks work because of his scholarship agreement. In addition, Mohammad Saeed had signed him up for the Muslim Educational Seminar to be held at the London Central Mosque the second week of the winter break in the evenings of Monday through Thursday. Jamil had heard of the London Central Mosque because it could hold five thousand worshipers at one time. In addition, because the students were off the during break, Jamil learned that the International Interfaith Council had scheduled a program for the students on Friday morning before prayers entitled "Middle East Issues" which he planned to attend.

According to his scholarship Jamil was to report to the Scholarship Office on the Monday morning after school recessed. When he did, he realized that there were a large number of other students there for the same meeting. Being a few minutes early, he sat down to wait.

Adopted or the lawyer's son?

At the meeting he learned the group had been divided into "odd" and "even" sections based on whether the day of your birthday was odd or even. He found himself in the "even" group. They all learned that for Monday through Thursday in week one the "odd" group was volunteering at King's College Hospital Children's Ward to help with and entertain the children. Monday through Thursday "even" group was to report to King's College Maintenance Department to help with painting dorm rooms and doing other needed upkeep work. In week two, the groups reversed jobs.

On Friday of the first week, the groups were together for a discussion on the topic of "How to Best Help the Poor of Asia and Africa." The discussion was to be led by a faculty member knowledgeable about the topic being discussed. The idea was to raise the student's awareness of important socioeconomic and political issues.

Jamil had never done painting and maintenance work before and for the first couple of days found it interesting as he learned. He quickly discovered that very soon they all became well qualified painters, the work was monotonous and not something he would want to do even for a summer job if he could avoid it.

Adopted or the lawyer's son?

Paint, paint, swish, swish.

Adopted or the lawyer's son?

Paint, paint, swish, swish.

Adopted or the lawyer's son?

At the Friday discussion session he quickly learned that his lack of micro- and macro-economics and history hampered his understanding of the important issues. There were students who had the academic background and/or who had experienced the poor economic and health conditions of Asia and Africa. Many had existed on one meal a day. They were very fortunate for the scholarships they received because it was their best ticket out of those wretched conditions. Jamil quickly realized that their scholarships had actually benefited him as well since he had no other good way of learning these topics. Without the background others had, he could not participate as fully, and his mind quickly drifted to more immediate and important concerns such as the girl in biology and.... Adopted or the lawyer's son?

The second week was more interesting. He felt sorry for the children in the hospital but realized that they were there because of some disease or condition and would be healthier when they had completed their treatments. He was pleased to assist in helping the children. Unlike the maintenance work, with the children he had to keep his mind on what he was doing.

The Monday night of the second week was the beginning of the Muslim Educational Seminar. Starting time was 19:00, but he arrived a little early to tour the mosque and learn the week's schedule. He found out that each night was a separate program which ran three hours. The schedule was:

> Monday—Why Muslims Who Promote Jihad
>   Against the West Misinterpret The Qur'an
> Tuesday—Economic Issues Facing Muslims

> Wednesday—Why Muslims Who Promote
> Jihad Against the West Correctly Interpret
> The Qur'an
> Thursday—Self Defense and Military Matters

As he reviewed the program, he thought all the topics were of interest to him, but particularly the programs on Monday and Wednesday. He had always wondered how two reasonable people could read the same "good book" and come up with such very different ideologies; now I will learn. Jamil was familiar with some of the interpretations of the New and Old Testaments where some believe the world is about 6,000 years old and others believe it is 4 or 5 billion years old. Further, that some interpret the commandment, "Thou Shall Not Kill/Murder" to mean there should be no death penalty while others believe that the commandment does not apply to those convicted of having taking a life; after all, "An eye for an eye!"

On Monday Jamil was not disappointed. From the beginning, the speaker addressed the issue of different interpretations of the Qur'an. He said, "The phenomenon of having different interpretations for the same text, be it scripture or not, is very common, and is probably the norm. The difference is that some people who read scriptures use their interpretation to justify certain preconceived attitudes and behavior. Since the 'original author' is not readily available to correct the reader's interpretation or provide the right interpretation, these people can carry out their 'validated' behavior thinking and believing that they are doing the 'right' thing; that which the Qur'an authorized." That was consistent with what Jamil had observed.

The speaker continued, "Now I want to explain why Islam is a peaceful religion and why our 'good book,' the Qur'an, teaches peaceful coexistence with those who live in peace and are respectful of us. The Qur'an, by the consensus of all Muslims, contains the literal word of God and thus is the ultimate reference in determining what is acceptable and what is not. Even the command to follow the footsteps of our prophet Muhammad (peace be upon him) and his tradition came from the Qur'an."

Without dropping a beat, the speaker went on. "The Qur'an, (3:7), contains two kinds of verses. First are verses *muhkamat*—those that can only be interpreted in one way—and are usually related to the articles of faith and the Unity of God, and the Hereafter, and second are verses *mutashabeehat* which linguistically can be interpreted in more than one way. It is the presence of these two kinds of verses that makes the Qur'an valid and compatible for all generations in different times and places. It makes the important and critical aspect of Islam fixed and stable, and allows certain details and minor issues to have ample variability (within a certain framework of acceptable Islamic validation) to accommodate change over time and place."

Jamil listened intently as the speaker continued, "Unlike Christianity, Islam does not recognize a hierarchy in a church establishment or priesthood. We do recognize the presence of scholars who have devoted their time and effort in studying the Islamic tradition from its primary sources and have shown, over the years, noble and righteous character that fit their level of knowledge. These well-known scholars, and by the way Osama bin Laden and Ayman al Zawahiri are definitely not considered Islamic scholars, are the ones who are capable and eligible to make interpretation of ambiguous verses of the Qur'an or make a 'fatwa' about issues that are not clearly stated in the Qur'an or the Sunna (the tradition of the prophet Muhammad, peace be upon him)."

"Regarding the relation between Muslims and the People of the Book (Jews and Christians), there is no single verse in the entire Qur'an that states, implicitly or explicitly, that Muslims have to kill them. In fact, verse (5:5) allows Muslim men to marry a woman from the People of the Book as long as she believes in the Unity of God. So it would not be logically acceptable for one verse to allow a Muslim to marry a Jew or a Christian, then in another verse order you to kill your own wife. There are numerous verses in the Qur'an that talk about the People of the Book (especially the children of Israel, also known as B'nai Israel), knowing that Jesus was also Jewish and their history and their relationship with their different prophets. Moses is the prophet who is mentioned more than any other prophet in the Qur'an. If you read carefully these verses, you might find some generalization about their character and attitude, but almost always you will find exception about their nobility and righteous character (2:83, 3:55-58, 3:64, 3:75, 3:113-115, 3:199)."

"The Qur'an and the tradition of the prophet Muhammad have taught us to seek, promote and live in peace with ourselves, with our Creator, and with our fellow man, regardless of their ethnic or religious background. Islam does not coerce or impose its teaching on anyone (2:256, 18:29). Yet, it does not allow transgression or oppression to occur, and encourages Muslims to oppose any form of oppression or abuse; hence, the notion of Jihad that allows Muslims to defend themselves or their land. But even during military Jihad (since Jihad has different forms and ways) Muslims are only allowed to engage with combatants and prevent any engagement with civilians, especially religious people, women and children." He noted that this was unlike what was happening in a number of places in the Middle East and Asia. The goal of any war involving Muslims—and, by the way, there is nothing called 'Holy war' in Islam — is to break the vicious cycle of oppressed-oppressor that can lead to more bloodshed and wars (the idea of the Israelis killing the Palestinians because they were killed by the Germans)."

Jamil thought the speaker had finished, but after a pause, he continued, "The Qur'an recognizes that every one lived in unity in the beginning (2:213), but humans are created different and have different talents and ways to perceive and run their lives. These different ways should be complementary and don't have to be contradictory to each other. The Qur'an encourages people to know each other, respect their different ways and learn how to effectively and synergistically live together and tolerate each other while recognizing their differences (49:13)."

At this conclusion most of the attendees stood and applauded in support of what they heard. There were a few who applauded politely and did not stand. To Jamil it seemed that they were being polite but were not enthusiastic about what they had heard. He concluded that they might be the ones more interested in the Wednesday lecture.

On Tuesday Jamil learned that according to the average Muslim around the world, he was very well educated and considered wealthy; so many unfortunately were uneducated and very poor.

Before Wednesday's program, Jamil had heard from some that were involved in sponsoring the program that the speaker would use the Qur'an to justify the attacks on the Cole and other U.S. assets as well as on Christians, Jews and other "infidels." He thought, regardless of how they want to justify those acts, I don't believe they are condoned by the Qur'an and I will just be upset that they put Islam in a bad light with regard to the non-Muslim world. There is no use in my attending; I can use my time in a more productive manner.

As he reflected on Monday's program when observing the attendees, Jamil realized that while many Muslims attending were Palestinian Arabs, that about an equal number were non-Arabs but were Asian. Jamil quickly realized in the past he had erroneously equated ethnicity with religion. He knew better, but somehow made the mistake. It was incorrect to equate Palestinian with Muslim and Israeli with Jew. With regard to religion, he recalled that many geopolitical disputes were religiously based; Northern Ireland (Catholic vs. Protestant) and Iraq (Sunni vs. Shiite), and India (Muslim vs. Hindu). Jamil's thoughts continued, if Islam does not have hostility towards Christians and Jews, then maybe the Middle East conflict is not a religious one between Muslims and Jews but rather an ethnic one between Palestinians and Israelis. His thoughts then took the next logical step, that the Middle East conflict maybe had nothing to do with ethnicity either. Could it be that it was just the simple case that the Israelis/Jews had a piece of land including a few very holy religious places which the Palestinians/Muslims regarded as their own and also wanted. It may well have nothing to do with the fact that the people who have the land were Israelis or Jews. Jamil realized that if other Arab/Muslims had taken land that he and his family had regarded as theirs, he would have been equally displaced. If Sunni Muslims had the land to the exclusion of Shiite Muslims, there would be conflict between Muslims, Sunni v. Shiite. If that is correct, then it is simply the fact that there is one Jerusalem and surrounding area with its holy places and two groups of people who want it. For centuries wars have been fought because one party had land that another wanted. Sometimes it had to do with religion or ethnicity. He recalled that in the United States, in 1776 the colonists fought England for what became the 13 colonies over taxation. Similarly when the colonists fought the Indians for lands in the west, land was the issue not religion nor ethnicity. The Middle East may simply be a situation of Group A having land that Group B wants. The more Jamil thought, the more sense that made to him. His spirit rose as the concept made more and more sense to him. Further, if he was correct it meant there was no inherent conflict between Muslims and Jews or Arabs and Israelis; it meant a peaceful resolution could be obtained by learning to share the land, in particular those places deemed holy by more than one religion. While Jamil was glad he had this chance for internal reflection, his new views left him uneasy. He thought it would be interesting subject matter to discuss with other Arabs and Muslims back on campus.

On Thursday Jamil learned that "Defense" included informing the participants of the various martial arts classes available to them and how they would help them protect themselves and their families if attacked. He was surprised to learn that the "Military Matters" were really offensive training for those who believed the Imam who spoke on Wednesday supporting jihad. As Jamil was going into the mosque for the Thursday program he ran into Mohammad Saeed.

"Mohammad, what are you doing here?"

"What do you think, trying to learn."

"But, having lived in London and being a senior at King's College I thought you would have taken this seminar before."

"You are right, I did. However, because of the importance of tonight's session, I thought I would come hear it again."

"What about tonight's session makes it so important to you?"

"You will see, let's go listen."

The leader began, "Suicide missions have been very successful for Islam over the past two decades such as the 18 April 1983 suicide bombing of the U.S. Embassy in Beirut which killed 60; the 23 October 1983 suicide bombing of the Beirut barracks killing 220 U.S. Marines; the 6 July 1989 Tel Aviv-Jerusalem bus attack by Abd al-Hadi Ghanayem; the 7 August 1998 suicide bombings of the U.S. embassies in Tanzania and Kenya killing hundreds, etc., etc. Now to continue to be on the offensive against the immoral society of the West, we need more individuals willing to put the Qur'an, Islam and our society above their own lives. We need volunteers willing to become martyrs. Those who volunteer will be heroes as martyrs. You are guaranteed a place in heaven where you will receive 72 virgins as a reward. In addition, your family will receive $25,000."

The leader continued, "It works best if we have two individuals who will work in pairs. You work sequentially, not simultaneously, with a very short period of time in between. The first bomber causes as many casualties as possible. Besides the casualties, the first blast attracts law enforcement, medical rescue workers, curious bystanders and the public who wants to be helpful. This also gives the second bomber easy access to a larger number of people. The arrangement usually works best if the pair are friends."

The leader then continued for those not considering being a suicide bomber but who wanted to learn how to use weapons for protection and war if it comes, we have various programs. He set forth various places to learn the different weapons available. None of this interested Jamil and he was tempted to leave but since Mohammad was sitting next to him, he thought it not polite to stand up and leave. It did not interest Jamil because he thought the practice was counterproductive. First, the suicide bomber is lost. If he/she would just planted a bomb or shot a few people, he/she could escape and strike again, again and again and be more effective than just one hit. Second, all the hundreds or thousands who have given their lives could make a good size army. Third, he thought the 72 virgins was a sly way to attract young men. Where do all the virgins come from? Isn't it against Islamic law to have sex outside of marriage? Does the bomber marry each of the 72 after divorcing the previous one? What would young female suicide bombers want with 72 virgins? Do they get 72 virgin men? When the program was over and they were leaving, Jamil asked Mohammad, "Are you seriously considering it?"

"No, no...not really. In the states $25,000 may not be a considerable sum, but to my family in Gaza it would be a vast fortune. I was also tempted by the idea of the 72 virgins. Someone like me would never have any experience like that here. I know my parents, brothers, sister and grandmother certainly could use the money. Now they are trying to help me finish school. Fortunately, I have two scholarships; but I still work to make ends meet.

When I finish college I could send them money, but that will not be for a couple of years. In addition, I have five younger siblings some of whom would like the opportunity to go to college. My parents have done a lot for me and I would like to help them if I can. But... no... no... not really."

"I'm glad to hear that. Let's stop and have some hot chocolate on the way back to campus."

"Good idea."

Because he thought the Friday morning program by the International Interfaith Council on Middle East Issues would be particularly good Jamil arrived early to get a good seat.

A very distinguished elderly gentleman wearing a traditional India turban rose and slowly began to speak.

"I am Gadhadhar the Executive Director of the International Interfaith Council and while the issue that we will be discussing pertains mostly to Muslims and Jews, I am neither. I am a Sikh from India. Our organization is a coalition of members of virtually all faiths. While religion can be a tremendous force for good in the world it also has been the impetus for much conflict, oppression and even wars. It is readily apparent from observing that two different individuals can read the same Old Testament with regard to the appropriate punishment for capital murder and some will cite "an eye for an eye" while others will point to "thou shall not kill" that the 'good books' of the world are subject to many different and sometimes conflicting interpretations. The International Interfaith Council's vision is two part, first to make sure the people of the world can practice their faith or religion as they wish without government interference. Second and equally important, is to have the religions recognize that while they should have the freedom to practice their religion as they wish, they should not try to force their beliefs on others as others also want the freedom to practice their faith as they wish. Our code implicitly includes respect for those who have no religious belief."

"At this time I would like to introduce our speaker but he is not here! I apologize; this has never happened before at any of our programs. About an hour ago I received a call from him that weather delayed his flight here and he will be a little late. While we are waiting for him I would to take this opportunity to get to know your thoughts on the Middle East. Please keep your comments brief and to the issue of the Middle East, in particular what can be done now to permit all of Abraham's descendents to live peacefully with each other in the Middle East as they do in other places in the world.

The gentleman in the third row with the blue jacket. "Because Zionism is racism, Israel's existence is illegitimate and the US should stop ..."

"That is crazy. Israel is a legitimate country created by ..."

"Stop. Let the gentleman finish. You may not like what he is saying, but he has the right to speak. You can have your chance to respond. Sir, please finish."

"As I was saying, Israel's existence is illegitimate and the US should stop funding Israeli's apartheid. Without US funding, Israel would cease to exist and the Palestinians would be able to reclaim the land which is theirs. This occurs because the Jews in the US control the banks and money therefore they control US policy. That policy is to further their own selfish economic interests. Israel is prospering and the people in the Palestinian territory are starving because of the wall separating Israel and Palestine and the blockade of Gaza prohibiting needed supplies from getting to the Palestinians and the Palestinians from exporting anything."

"I will give the individual who interrupted a chance to respond."

"Israel was duly created by the UN. His accusation regarding racism is easily disproven in view of the fact that hospitals in Israel take care of both Arabs and Israelis, Muslims, Jews, Christians and anyone else. They even have an Arab/Muslim on their Supreme Court. I doubt that a Jew holds any governmental position in any of the Palestinian territories."

"The lady over there with the books in her hand."

"I am old enough to be the grandmother of the previous speaker and have lived in Middle East most of my life. Generally, I support what the speaker said. I can understand the Israelis wanting a homeland, but so do we. [Applause] There have been a number of 'agreements' but the Israelis never will fulfill the terms, they keep breaking ..."

"It is the not Israel that breaks the agreements but the Palestinians who break the agreements by ..."

"Stop it! After this, would the security detail please immediately remove anyone in the room who interrupts anyone else? If they don't go peacefully, drag them out. I will not tolerate these interruptions. If you can't even discuss issues civilly, how do you ever expect to negotiate a peaceful settlement?"

"Would the lady please continue?"

"There have been a number of agreements but the Israelis never will fulfill the terms, they keep breaking the treaties because they have the support of the US. They do what they want without repercussions from the US. Many US Presidents have been frustrated with the Israelis and their leadership but do nothing because the Jews control the US monetary system."

"Would the young man want to respond?"

"Yes. I apologize for interrupting but what she was saying is totally untrue. It is the Palestinians who break the agreements by not being willing to recognize Israel as the Jewish state with its capital in Jerusalem and continuing to support terrorists by permitting them to shoot rockets into Israel from Gaza."

"I am hearing complaints but nothing regarding what can be done so the Israelis and Palestinians can live together peacefully. The gentleman over there with the tie and suit."

"It is amazing to hear complaints of being unable to make peace with Israel. How can anyone expect Israel to make peace with the Palestinians when they actively supported so many suicide bombers that Israel had to put up the wall to protect its citizens and the Palestinians do not do anything to prevent rockets from being shot from Gaza into Israel?"

"Again, I am hearing complaints of old conduct but nothing about moving forward. The student with the bright green backpack."

"What the previous speakers presented is exactly the plan set forth in *The Protocols of the Elders of Zion* a book which describes the Jewish plan to take over the world by controlling the world's money and economics. What we are seeing now is what the book discloses to be the Jewish aim. This is not just some fabricated story, it has been translated into many languages and was distributed as early as the 1920s in the US and is all over the internet."

"We have heard this charge many many times and have investigated it thoroughly. The fact that it is on the internet and the book has been translated does not alter that it is fiction. There is plenty on the internet indicating that man has never landed on the moon. That does not make it true. We are not getting anywhere. You all make accusations which even *if* true have no one to adjudicate a remedy for you. Does anyone have a suggestion for moving forward?"

"I do."

"Good. Let's hear it."

"First a statement of facts, then my proposal. Hamas was founded in 1988 to liberate Palestine from Israeli occupation and to establish an Islamic state in the area that is now Israel including the West Bank and the Gaza Strip. Its charter calls for the eventual creation of an Islamic state in Palestine and the obliteration or dissolution of Israel. Hezbollah is a Muslim militant group and political party based in Lebanon. Hezbollah's 1985 manifesto listed as one of its four main goals 'Israel's final departure from Lebanon as a prelude to its final obliteration.' Its leaders have also made numerous statements calling for the destruction of the state of Israel. I suggest that if the Palestinians really want a peaceful two state solution, they renounce both Hamas and Hezbollah, recognize Israeli's right to exist as a Jewish state in exchange for a return to the 1965 borders and a sharing of Jerusalem."

"That is not unreasonable. Do you think Israel would return to the 1965 borders and share Jerusalem if it gets what it wants?"

"I think there is a good possibility."

"Does any wish to comment on this proposal?"

"I will. I don't think it is realistic. Israel will not share Jerusalem and the Palestinians will not renounce either Hamas or Hezbollah. Further, even a Jewish group, Jewish Voice for Peace, calls for an end to US aid to Israel because of Israel's apartheid policies. It supports divestment campaigns against Israel."

"I think the polarized attitudes of the audience are well demonstrated. This is one reason why progress is not made on this very complex problem. Each side would rather criticize and blame the other rather than put concrete proposals on the table for solving this problem. The note that was just handed to me informs me that our speaker has just arrived. When we get to questions, comments and answers, I am going to require that all questions and comments be prospective. If anyone reverts to retrospective criticism, I will request that security take the microphone from that person. Retrospective criticism will not solve the problem.

So I am absolutely clear on what I mean about discussing issues prospectively rather than retrospective criticism I will give an example using what has been discussed here. I hear that the Palestinians want the wall removed so it will be much easier to cross the border. They also want the blockade of Gaza ended so goods and people can come in and out. I hear the Israelis want a secure country recognized by the Palestinians meaning their borders and property are respected which would include suicide bombings stopping and no rockets being shot into the country. Instead of each side complaining about the other, realize if you want something from another party you have to give that party something they want in exchange. For example, would Israel take down the walls, end the blockade and permit Palestinians/Arabs to travel freely across the border between Palestine and Israel *if* the Palestinians would agree to recognize Israel as a Jewish independent country, do all they can to end military actions against Israel including stopping suicide bombings and rockets being shot into the country? Likewise, would the Palestinians recognize Israel as a Jewish independent country, do all they can to end military actions against Israel including stopping suicide bombings and rockets being shot into the country if Israel takes down the walls, ends the blockade and permits Palestinians/Arabs to travel freely across the border between Palestine and Israel."

"Our speaker just arrived. Since time is short because the speaker is late, I will limit my introduction to less than one minute so we can spend our time on his fascinating and intriguing path forward."

עשרים ושתיים

GOING TO HELP MY SISTER

To: JacobCA@gmail.com
From: Dr. Levine@IDF.org
Subject: Your sister
Date: 27 January 00

Your situation has been thoroughly reviewed. The decision is based on where your sister is, the time of the year in our training cycle, your personal skills and present position within the IDF.

First year trainees break for the summer in July and return on 15 August. Given the travel, your sister's condition and the opportunities in "the states," it best if you spend time with your sister, obtain some specialized training in the United States and return in time for our fall training. Because of your being gone for a few months, you need to be back here on 10 Aug at 10:00. Hence, the schedule is, you leave here on 3 February (we have your ticket to LAX) and help your sister during February and March. On 2 April you will take a 10-week course at the National Forensics Academy in Knoxville, Tennessee. You will specialize in intercepting wireless transmissions. We will provide you with the registration materials and other relevant information.

On 1 July you will report to the CIA in Langley, Virginia, for the month to learn Arabic and methods of monitoring Arabic websites and help them with Hebrew to the extent that they need or want help. This next item is very important; while at CIA, do not contact anyone at IDF and best not do much communicating with anyone, including your family. CIA will be monitoring your email and phone communications.

You can vacation with your family the first week of August. Since you must be back here on 10 August, we booked you on El Al flight LY12 on the morning of 9 August leaving from New York (JFK) to arrive at Ben Gurion International Airport (TLV) on 9 Aug at 17:15. You should easily be able to clear immigration and customs in time to catch Bus 81 at 20:00 from the airport to Jerusalem. We use this combined routing of air and bus often and it works well. Someone will pick you up at the bus station at 20:50.

Dr. Levine

To: Dr. Levine@IDF.org
From: JacobCA@gmail.com
Subject: Re: Your sister
Date: 27 January 00

Wow and thanks! That is great and I really appreciate it. I will be on Bus 81 on 9 August.

Please pass my appreciation on to those who made the decisions. I am sure my sister would have done the same for me and I want to give her the bone marrow if I match.

Jacob

To: Sarah.Goodman@yahoo.com;
    JennyCA@gmail.com
From: JacobCA@gmail.com
Subject: Coming Home
Date: 27 January 00

Things worked out great here. I arrive LAX on AA 3451 on 3 February at 9:45 pm.

How is Jenny doing?

I am free to do whatever is needed until I have to be in Knoxville on 2 April. There I receive United States government training until the end of July. I can spend the first week of August with the two of you but must leave on 9 August from NY to return here.

Not only I am not penalized for leaving, I will receive some specialized training in the states. See you in a few days.

Love, Jacob

To: JacobCA@gmail.com
From: Sarah.Goodman@yahoo.com
Subject: Re: Coming Home
Date: 29 January 00

I will be at LAX to pick you up.

Jenny is not doing well. She is getting weaker and she has an infection that she is having trouble fighting off. The doctors are convinced she needs a bone marrow replacement. I offered mine but they told Jenny they prefer to use yours, if you are a match, since you are younger.

She has a doctor's appointment on 4 February in San Diego. You will be tested at that time. Have a good flight back, I know it is a l-o-o-o-ong way.

Thank everyone there in the IDF from both of us.

Love, Mom

Abraham's Tears

Twenty-three
AND THE WINNER IS . . .

When 1 March 00 arrived, everyone was waiting in anticipation for the drawing which was conducted by Pastor Fitzgerald. Pastor Fitzgerald began, "I want someone who is under age 10 to do the drawing. Is there anyone here who is under 10 and having a birthday today? No one? Anyone who had a birthday last week? Marci, good. Please come up here. Marci, I want you to put your hand in the box and pull out just one ticket without looking. OK? Good."

"And the winner is ticket #288642, Elizabeth Dodson. I don't recognize that name. Is she a new member?"

"Woopie! Pastor, Elizabeth Dodson, is my sister. She is not here today for some reason. I will be happy to call her and tell her she won. She and Eugene will be ecstatic. Outstanding, I don't think she ever won anything before in her life."

Abraham's Tears

Vierundzwanzig
TRAVEL IS AUGUST 8th

To: GoldbergAD@gmail.com
From: HBerniseWECB@gmail.com
Subject: Re: Our Meeting
Date: 6 June 00

Dr. Goldberg:

I am unavailable on the 7th, but can arrive on August 8th to meet on the 9th.

Hans

Abraham's Tears

خمسة وعشرون

ISRAELI–ARAB CONFLICT— ANALYZED

Gadhadhar continued, "The International Interfaith Council has thoroughly studied virtually all religious conflicts including the recent one in Northern Ireland between Catholics and Protestants because we want to learn what causes the conflicts so we can help resolve those and prevent others. Our goal is to help the various religions of the world live peacefully together. With regard to the Middle East conflict, Professor Spivak's papers and presentations shows that he approaches solving the Middle East situation in a very pragmatic way which has not been presented by others that we are aware of nor immediately apparent. For that reason, the International Interfaith Council has selected him as the best person to help us resolve the Middle East situation. I give you Professor Spivak."

"Thank you for the very kind introduction. In order to try and settle the Middle East situation between Israel and the Palestinians, one first needs to learn the cause of the conflict. Exactly what is it that is causing the conflict between the Palestinians/Muslims/Arabs and the Israelis/Jews on the issue of Israel/Palestine? Other than the issue of Israel and Jerusalem, Muslims and Jews don't appear to have an apparent religious or other ethnic conflict. There is no direct or indirect religious conflict in the Jewish Bible or Qur'an. For example, if Muslims can't get halal food they are instructed by many Muslim leaders to get kosher food. Muslims and Jews live and work side by side in many areas of the world without conflict, such as the Detroit suburbs where there are large numbers of both groups. Why the conflict in Israel?"

"The conventional wisdom or reasons are first religion and second ethnicity. However, I respectfully dissent. I will explain why."

"First the religious perspective.

If we look at the situation of Israel and the Palestinian area, the situation is the Israelis/Jews are in control of Israel and Jerusalem and the Palestinians do not have a country of their own. While it is tempting to think the problem is that Muslims and Jews cannot get along or have some inherent animosity that is incorrect. First, there is nothing in either of their religious books that requires to even suggest hostility between the two religions. Second, and probably more relevant to today's situation, what if the Israelis/Jews became tired of all the hassle and killing and sold Israel including Jerusalem to another interested religious party with the funds to buy it, say the Catholic Church. Further suppose the Israelis/Jews having sold Israel pack up and use their new fortune to purchase land far away and move there. I believe the same problem would exist for Muslims, they would still be on the outside and no longer be at war with Israelis/Jews, but now would be at war with Catholics, not because of any religious difference between Muslims and Catholics but because the Catholics would now control the things that the Israelis used to control and that the

Muslims still want. The same thing would happen if the Bahai religion controlled Israel/Jerusalem and the Muslim holy places. Muslims would be at war with the Bahais, not because of their religion but because again they would control something that the Muslims want control over. Does that make any sense to you? I would like a show of hands of those who believe this is probably correct. About 70%, good."

Professor Spivak continued, "It becomes more apparent when we look at ethnicity. What if the country Israel, including all the holy places, was owned and controlled not by Israelis but by Swedes or Chinese? Would Arabs be any happier to have control of the land and holy places in the hands of the Swedes or Chinese (who officially practice no religion)? I think not."

"The gentleman in the second row has his hand up. Maybe has an answer."

"I am a Muslim from Egypt and went to undergraduate school in Lebanon. I am here as a graduate student. To me it would be the same; it makes no difference if it is the Israelis, Swedes, Chinese or Martians that control our land including Jerusalem. To me the critical thing is that we, Muslims, would not have control."

Professor Spivak continued, "Exactly. Then it does not matter if the occupier of the land and the religious places are Israelis, Swedes or Martians. Therefore, the problem of the Middle East is neither a religious nor ethnic one. I will repeat that because I am sure it is something that you never heard before and even now are having trouble accepting regardless of whether you are a Jew, a Muslim or neither. The problem is simply someone else has the land that Palestinians want. To them it is a matter of justice. That someone else who just happens to have the land are the Israelis and they happen to be Jewish."

Professor Spivak paused for this new way of looking at the Middle East conflict to sink in and then went on, "If true, then Muslims have no inherent conflict with Jews over religion and Arabs have no inherent conflict with Israelis regarding ethnicity. Again the problem comes back to the situation that the Israelis who happen to be Jews have control over something that Arab/Muslims want. The Israelis let Muslims use the Temple Mount including the Dome of the Rock and the Al Aqsa Mosque, but the Israelis own it and make the rules. If the parties involved would recognized there is no inherent religious or ethnic conflict it should be much easier for the Palestinians and Israelis to share."

Professor Spivak paused to let audience wrestle in their brains with what does he mean by 'share' and then continued.

"It is apparent that both the Israelis/Jews and Palestinian/Muslims want certain land and holy places, in and around Jerusalem, the Tomb of the Patriarchs in Hebron, etc. In addition, the Tomb is also sacred to Christians which is an added problem. Both Jews and Muslims cannot exclusively control these places; if either has them, the other will want them. Hence, continuous hostilities unless the leaders of both groups realize that peaceful sharing is much better than the tragic continuous war. In that situation both groups would get some, but not all, of what they want. But hopefully the leaders of both groups will realize that peaceful sharing is better than the continuous hostilities. I see no reason why Jerusalem cannot be the capital for both nations."

The Professor continued, "What *if* Israel was to deed title to Old Jerusalem and the holy places in Jerusalem and Hebron to Abraham, then neither Israelis nor Palestinians, Muslims nor Jews would own them. Since they are all children of Abraham, he seems like an appropriate landlord. Next, what if it was decided that administration of the holy places was to be done by the religion(s) associated with those places? For example, if Christians were to be given sole responsibility for administering the Church of the Nativity, the Church of the Holy Sepulchre and say the Chapel of the Ascension, would Muslims or Jews complain? Probably not, because they have no real interest in those places. In fact, that is the present situation as Israel has given control over the Christian sites to the Christian churches. Similarly, if Jews were given sole control over the Wailing Wall or Joseph's Tomb would Muslims or Christians complain, probably not.

That leaves the Temple Mount which contains the Foundation Stone and Well of Souls and is covered by the Dome of the Rock. Just south of there on the Temple Mount is the Al Aqsa Mosque. Jews believe The Foundation Stone is the holiest place because from there God expanded the earth to its present form; that God gathered dust from the stone to form the first man, Adam; the binding of Isaac by Abraham took place there; the first and second temples were built there; when the first temple was built, it was the spot that the Ark of the Covenant stood (some believe it was located in the Well of Souls) and it is where the third and final temple will be built. Muslims regard the Temple Mount as the third holiest place in Islam (behind Mecca and Medina) because it is were Mohammad ascended to and from heaven during the Night Journey. Because it is the holiest place for Jews and third holiest for Muslims both want control of it. Presently the Israelis have control but permit Muslims to use and control the Temple Mount. Because it is so holy to Jews, they do not go there."

"Because the Temple Mount, Tomb of the Patriarchs, etc are holy to more than one religion Jews and Muslims should share these places and do so by joint administration."

A voice shot out of the audience, "Be real. You don't really think Israel would actually give up control and share by jointly administering places of common interest with Palestinians, do you?"

"Yes, if Palestinians/Muslims were willing to do so because if the Israelis did that, along with some other less controversial stuff, Palestinians/Muslims would have pretty much what they wanted, it might end the fighting and bring peace to the region. Therefore, agreeing to give sole administration of Muslim holy sites to Muslims and share administration of sites holy to more than one religion might be the key to bringing peace to the area."

This time Jamil was skeptical. "I don't think Arab/Muslims will co-administer with Israeli/Jews, I just don't."

"Why not? If they are to have two states side by side living in peace, they will have to agree to work together on much more than that, including such critical issues as defense, water, border crossings, etc.

"How will we know that the Israelis will keep their part of the bargain and give up 50% control and truly co-administer?"

"Good point. How do the Israelis know that the Palestinians will keep their part of the bargain? It is not only in the Israelis' and Palestinian's interest to solve the problems of the Middle East and live peacefully, but also in the world's interest. It would be nice to have organizations like the UN, NATO and the Arab League guarantee the agreement by enforcing it.

An elderly gentlemen who appeared to be of Scandinavian descent spoke up, "I don't have any horse in this race, but that sounds reasonable."

Professor Mughazy interjected, "I wish it were that simple. There is something about the devil being in the details. Both sides are skeptical of the neutrality of the organizations, and the positions of various countries change with changing governments."

Professor Spivak continued, "I believe that the key issue to solving the entire problem is how to generate trust."

Another voice came from the audience, "Wait, wait a minute. Even if the Israeli and Palestinian leaders learn to trust each other and work together, there is still a big problem. Professor Spivak, if there was a negotiated settlement, you and I could live next door to each other without a problem. However, you forget there are groups like Hamas and Hezbollah that not only kill Israelis but also intimidate and kill Palestinians who support living peacefully with Israel."

"No, I haven't forgotten about the terrorists. Besides the Palestinian hardliners there are also many Israelis who don't want Israel to negotiate at all with the Palestinians and certainly don't want Israel to give the Palestinians any land, in particular part of Jerusalem, or rights to religious places. Yes, you are absolutely correct - there is strong right wing opposition, both vocal and militant, on both sides, but more on the Palestinian side."

Before the Professor could continue a question came from the audience, "How do you expect to overcome those major obstacles?"

Professor Spivak paused while he looked out the window to observe the flakey snow lazily drifting down reflecting light from the almost full moon. "I have found," he said, "that with virtually all political issues there are three groups; those against, those for and those in the middle. Those for or against are usually ideologically driven and their minds often cannot be changed. Those in the middle usually represent a substantial group and they generally don't know enough to take a position, don't care or both. The important thing is that often it is this middle group that controls the outcome. Let me give you an example. In the United States prior to 1954, with regard to race, schools were "separate but equal." Then *Brown v. Board of Education* – which I'm sure you Poli-Sci people are familiar with – ruled 9-0 that 'separate educational facilities are inherently unequal.' Some supported the decision, many opposed it and at the time most of those in the middle opposed it."

"In the 50s, 60s and 70s many schools with primarily whites did all they could to prevent integration. The same people also strongly resisted integration of society in general. The Ku Klux Klan, not unlike Hamas and Hezbollah, terrorized blacks and the whites who helped or supported blacks. A number of cities in the South closed their community swimming pools rather than integrate them. Freedom Riders supporting equal rights for blacks were set upon and beaten by those opposed to integration and were often supported directly or indirectly by the police. A number were even murdered. Some states made it a crime for black and white to marry.

So it took years of litigation and education but the non-ideologues of the middle group slowly moved from supporting segregation to supporting integration. During that period the Ku Klux Klan went from a popular organization to nonexistent. The ideologues on each side are still there, some in the South still fly the Confederate Flag as a symbol of resistance, but the middle group has moved strongly from the conservative side of the issue to the liberal side.

One other thing that contributed to the swing is the proposition that older individuals tended to be comfortable with the status quo, segregation. As they aged and left the political arena and were replaced by younger players with out all the historical baggage who looked at the situation more objectively and concluded that race should not be an issue, the momentum moved to acceptance.

What happened with regard to race is not an isolated situation. Virtually the same thing happened with the abortion issue. In the United States, prior to 1973 abortion was generally made illegal by each state. Then in 1973, in *Roe v. Wade*, the United States Supreme Court ruled 7-2 that a woman had a constitutional right to an abortion. There are those who still oppose the ruling and keep trying to restrict a woman's right. Here again education and the changing demographics has led to more acceptance and support for the decision than in 1973. I see the same happening with regard to the two state solution."

Professor Spivak looked up to again to monitor the snow flakes and then at the faces of those around him and noticed none had fallen asleep, as some did during his lectures, but seemed interested so he continued. "Why all this history? Because I expect the same process to happen in the Middle East. There are groups on both sides of this issue in Israel as well as in the Arab world. The group in the middle is more accustomed to separation, accusing the other of provocations and continued warfare rather than peace and cooperation. However, I am convinced that the group in the middle will see the benefits of cooperation and living peacefully. Over time I believe they will learn not to fear each other, realize that they all want the same things for their families - peace, a job, a good school for their kids, clean and sufficient water, and a place to worship without the fear of bombs or rockets or other harassment."

"I believe in due time those in the middle group will be supportive of this and make it a success. There will always be those on both sides who are opposed and continue to resist. However, as time goes on those opposed will decrease in number and those supporting will increase. The important thing is to get it started. It will gradually grow as more see it working. It will snowball much as the snow out there is beginning to accumulate."

A female voice with a heavy accent from the back asked, "Assuming you are correct with regards to the long term, and I am not sure you are, why do you think a two state solution or negotiated sharing will succeed in the short term?"

"Look at it this way. Israel going it alone has existed in spite of Hamas and Hezbollah for many, many years. If Israel has been able to handle Hamas and Hezbollah by themselves, certainly Israel working with the moderate Arabs/Muslims would be able to do so. Just doing that for a few years will win over many of the undecided or skeptical Arabs and Israelis. Over the years the slow change in demographics will also be a positive factor."

At this point Gadhadhar moved to the podium. This is an excellent discussion and I mean discussion not lecture. You, the audience, have fully participated and your input is crucial to our reaching a final proposal which we believe is workable for all parties. It is Friday and Muslim prayers will start shortly. It is also the Jewish Sabbath starting at sundown. Because of the interest in this issue and the large number of both Muslims and Jews in the audience, we will take a break until after Friday prayers and then meet in room 107 of the Thatcher Building, which is just next door, until just before the Sabbath for further discussion. I am looking forward to it.

Abraham's Tears

עשרים ושש

SURPRISE

When the pilot said, "If those of you on the right side of the aircraft will look out the window you will see an awesome sight, the Grand Canyon," Jacob knew he was not only at the end of a long journey, he was almost "home."

As soon as he landed, he turned on his cell phone and heard a message from a familiar voice. "I am here at the airport circling. When you have your bags, give me a call." Mom was always there.

Without any medical training, Jacob could tell Jenny was quite ill. She tried to respond to him but seemed to have less energy than her 99-year old grandmother, Gertrude.

Jacob tried to be positive and reassuring, "Jenny, just relax and let mom and I take care of things. You will start receiving treatment in just two days."

Once she and her son were alone, Sarah lowered her voice and spoke pointedly. "Jacob, I am not sure you fully understand. On the 4th they will just test you to see if you are a match and they will give Jenny a transfusion to help her along. Even if you are a match, and there is no guarantee, they must pre-treat her with radiation or chemotherapy to destroy her sick bone marrow. So it may be some time before she actually is given new bone marrow. Also, not all family members will be a match, not even mothers!"

Jacob said, "Well, Jenny has two chances with the closest two people to her to find a match. Just by chance, one of us should be a match. What time should the three of us leave on the 4th?"

"You have driven to San Diego so many times you know how long it takes better than I. Just leave an extra 30 minutes to arrive at the hospital at once you turn off I-5 for UCSD. I could not leave work to go with the two of you. Originally I had it arranged but Betty's mother passed away yesterday and earlier this morning Todd quit to take a job with McKenzie Bakery. I called the hematology lab to see if I could have the blood test here but they were insistent that the blood analysis had to be done by them comparing my sample with Jenny's. They said I could have the blood drawn here, kept on ice and you could bring it there for analysis as long as you keep it in a cooler. So I went to Dr. Sassaman's office and they drew two tubes of blood that you need to take with you; they are in the refrigerator. Also this way I can save my vacation time for the bone marrow procedure and the follow up where Jenny will probably need me more."

Having attended UCSD, Jacob was familiar with the two-hour drive. He had to continue on I-5 to I-8 and then go east a couple of miles to the hospital. Jenny slept most of the way. When she was able, she told him that she had dropped soccer and was having trouble finding energy for school. She wanted to complete the semester so she would graduate and take the scholarship at the University of Michigan.

Surprise

Jacob found Scripps Mercy Hospital without a problem, parked and followed Jenny to the hematology lab. Jenny knew the path all too well.

Once they were finished with their procedures, they had lunch. Afterwards they were called into Dr. Cohen's office. "Dr. Cohen, I would like you to meet my brother, Jacob. He came here to be tested as a possible donor. We also brought two tubes of my mother's blood for testing."

"Hello, Jacob, nice to meet you. Jenny, how have you been doing since we met last?"

"I am more tired and then had the infection and fever that I called you about. I don't feel as strong as when I was here two weeks ago."

"That is understandable. We will start you on a transfusion shortly which should help. I have the results from the hematology lab and would like to discuss that with you. I was supposed to receive the results of your blood test, your brother's and your mother's."

"I gave blood, they took only one tube. Jacob gave two tubes I believe, and we brought two tubes of my mother's blood that was drawn two days ago in LA and kept in the refrigerator at home and then on ice during the trip down here."

"Mmmmmm. There is some mistake some place. I know your blood values from all the tests we have done here. Your mother is not here, but we have her blood and we have the two tubes Jacob just gave. Jacob, I would appreciate it if you would go back down to the lab and give them one more tube of blood for additional testing. I will call the lab and tell them what I want. OK?"

"Sure, I will give another tube if you need it. What happened?"

"Some mix-up. Fortunately, we caught it. No problem, just give them one more tube and then the two of you come back at about 3:00. No, let's be more efficient. Jenny, why don't you go and have your transfusion while they are re-testing Jacob's blood. When you are done, I would like both of you to come back and see me."

Jacob went and gave another blood sample and then went to keep Jenny company while she got her transfusion. When she was done, he asked, "Do you really feel different now?"

"Oh, yes. It's the difference between going to bed exhausted and waking up partially-rested. Let's go and learn the results from Dr. Cohen."

"Good, I'm glad you are feeling better." Then Jacob began to sing, "Matchmaker, matchmaker, make me a match."

Jenny laughed and quickly added, "I hope your blood is better than your singing!"

When they arrived back at Dr. Cohen's office, the receptionist told them that Dr. Cohen needed to speak to them separately and he wanted to talk to Jacob first.

"I am not sure where to begin, Jacob. We do many tests to check and see if someone is a suitable donor for a particular person. The first test, one of the oldest of its kind, is the simple blood type. There are four blood types - A, B, AB and O blood types, that is it. Your sister's blood type is A. We have two tubes of your mother's blood and she is AB. We have tested you twice and both tests show you are O."

Surprise

"So? So, I am O, so what?"

"A mother with a blood type AB cannot have a child with blood type O."

"What?"

"A woman with blood type AB, such as your mother, cannot have a son with a blood type O. It is impossible."

"Are you saying I am not my mother's son?"

"Yes."

"That's crazy. Your labs must have made another mistake. We have no secrets. If I were adopted or something she would have told me. "

"I know it is a shock. That is why I wanted to talk to you separately. It does not mean you may not be a match for Jenny. It is still possible that you can donate, we need to do the remaining tests. Your mother may be a suitable donor, we don't know yet. It takes 24 hours to run those tests."

"No. No. Something here must be wrong with your tests."

"We did not make a mistake. There is no question, you are blood type O."

"This is nuts. Wait a minute. Just wait. I need to make a call."

"Mom, this is Jacob and I'm with Dr. Cohen."

"Well?" she said.

"He doesn't know if either of us is a match yet, those results won't be back until tomorrow. However, he has the results of some of our other blood tests. He says our blood types are ... you are AB, Jenny is A. And I am O."

"So?" said Sarah. "So you're O."

"Yeah, I'm O, and Dr. Cohen tells me that a woman with blood type AB cannot have a son with a blood type O."

Jacob heard nothing from the other end of the phone for a couple of seconds, so he continued.

"He said that Jenny has been tested many times and he is sure she is A. The two tubes of your blood are from a different hospital and look different from theirs here, so they couldn't have been accidentally switched. The only mix-up could have been mine, so they retested me and Dr. Cohen himself ran the test the second time himself. He says there is no question, that I am blood type O, which means I could not be your son."

"He is correct."

"WHAT DO YOU MEAN HE IS CORRECT I am not your son?"

"I will explain fully tonight."

"What do you mean you will explain tonight. No, tell me now! What happened? Who are my biological parents? How did you come to raise me? Is Jenny my sister?"

"I am at work and have to go."

"I know you are at work. It isn't that complicated. Just tell me what happened! Who am I?"

"No, it is complicated and I will explain when you come home."

Surprise

"I don't want to wait, this is important, tell me now. No, don't hang up, tell me now."

Jacob slumped into the closest chair with a tear slowly running down his cheek like an icicle slowly beginning to melt in the spring. "Doc, you're right, I am not her son."

"I am sorry you had to learn this way. It was never my intent to cause a problem. Given all the blood testing and looking for a match for Jenny, you would have been told by someone very soon. I thought it best that I explain it to you now."

"It's such a shock. Up until a few minutes ago, I would have bet everything you were wrong."

"This is not uncommon, it has happened to us a number of times before. Please take a few minutes to calm yourself. What do you want to do about your sister finding out?"

"Please tell her; I don't think I can."

"Carol, will you send Jenny Goodman in please?"

"Jenny, please go in and have a seat."

"Jacob, what's wrong?"

"Listen."

"Jenny, you know you are blood type A. Your mother's blood samples showed her to be type AB. Your brother's showed him to be type O."

"So what, is that a problem?"

"The problem is that a woman with blood type AB can not have a child with blood type O; it is impossible."

"No, that can't be correct. Jacob is my brother, there must be some mistake."

"No, there is no mistake. This is one of the oldest and most well-known blood tests. There is no mistake."

"You're not my brother?"

"I was until a few minutes ago but not any more. I called mom. She verified that I am not but she would not tell me who my parents are or what happened. She said she will tell me when we get home."

"Oh no, wow, this is as much of a shock; probably not as much of a shock as it is to you. Maybe I am not her daughter either. Doctor, what about my blood type and my mother's?"

"A woman with AB blood type can have a child with either A, B or AB. All I can tell from the blood types is you may be her daughter but Jacob cannot be her son. I am sorry that this had to happen. We will know tomorrow if either Jacob or your mother is a suitable donor for you. If not, we will keep looking."

"Jenny, let's go home fast. I want to know what happened, who my parents are, why mom has me and has raised me. We can also find out if you are her daughter."

"Wait I want to call her and find out if I am her daughter."

"No, don't. She is at work and she told me she does not want to talk about it until we arrive home. Let's go now."

Twenty-seven
NOTIFYING ELIZABETH

"Eliz, guess what? You and Eugene won our church raffle! No I am not pulling your leg, your ticket was the one drawn; ticket #288642. I am so pleased for you. You and your kids will certainly have a great time. The Church will send you the details in the near future. Your tour starts there August 9th."

Abraham's Tears

Achtundzwanzig
MEETING ON AUGUST 9th

To: HBerniseWECB@gmail.com
From: GoldbergAD@gmail.com
Subject: Re: Our Meeting
Date: 8 June 00

Dr. Bernise:

Excellent. We will have a driver there to pick you up on August 8th and we can meet on the 9th and 10th. Please forward your flight schedule so our driver will know the airline and what time to meet you.

Aaron

Abraham's Tears

تســعة و عشـــرون

THE ANSWER

Following Friday prayers, Jamil attended the continuation of Professor Spivak's presentation but found that there was little new. It was mostly a rehash and argument of issues that were previously discussed.

Jamil was amazed as to how much he had learned in the few months he had been away from home. It was a great experience but he missed Fatima, Samira and Charles.

>To: Fatima.Mansour@yahoo.com; SamiraM@gmail.com
>From: JamilM@gmail.com
>Subject: Hi from the other side of the earth
>Date: 28 December 99
>
>>How are you doing? I miss both of you. I hope you have a great New Year and new century! My winter "vacation" was not a vacation. One week I worked doing boring maintenance including painting dorm rooms and the other week I helped with hospitalized children, which was a rewarding experience. We also had educational sessions including one on the Middle East and an evening seminar series. It was an excellent learning experience but too much to include

here. Next semester starts in a few days and after the vacation I am ready to go!

Love, Jamil

New Year's Day came and went and Jamil watched some of the football bowl games from the States that were televised in London. Because of the time difference, the games went into early the next morning of the next day. Neither Dave nor Hasan were much interested; they were interested in the soccer matches that were going on in Europe.

School started again—more English History, a new biology course, second semester math and now chemistry. Same old day-to-day routine. Then Jamil remembered.... Adopted or the lawyer's son?

January...
Monday, Tuesday, Wednesday, Thursday, Friday.
English History, Bio 134, Math 102, Chem 233.
Adopted or the lawyer's son?

February...
Monday, Tuesday, Wednesday, Thursday, Friday.
English History, Bio 134, Math 102, Chem 233.
Adopted or the lawyer's son?

March...

Monday, Tuesday, Wednesday, Thursday, Friday.

English History, Bio 134, Math 102, Chem 233.

Adopted or the lawyer's son?

April...
Monday, Tuesday, Wednesday, Thursday, Friday.
English History, Bio 134, Math 102, Chem 233.
Adopted or the lawyer's son?

May...

The Answer

Monday, Tuesday, Wednesday, Thursday, Friday.
English History, Bio 134, Math 102, Chem 233.
Adopted or the lawyer's son?

One weekend in May as the sun was going down, Jamil was at the ocean's edge thinking only two weeks left until I go home. Then I will have my answer; but will it make any difference? Probably not. I can only guess; I have no idea which. As the sun began to hide behind the waves, he realized that in a few hours it would be rising on his home which made him more lonely. He jokingly thought, maybe I can grab the sun's tail and hitch a ride home! He realized he should promptly finalize his plans for returning home. His last final was on May 27th and he booked his flight for May 28th. He realized he would miss Dave and Hasan, especially Hasan; it was like having a brother.

Adopted or the lawyer's son?

As Delta Air Lines flight 5 descended into Detroit Metro, Jamil began to feel a sense of anticipation. He had narrowed the possibilities. His anticipation was peaking.

Once on the ground, he activated his cell phone to let Fatima know he had landed. Fatima answered and he was relieved. Before he could say anything, she let him know that she was not at the airport but his sister had just left to pick him up. It would take him time to go through both Immigration and Customs. She said once his sister reached the airport she would circle in the car and wait for him to call her and tell her what gate he would come out of. Jamil realized there was no quick way to go through Immigration, especially being an Arab even though he had a United States passport. As soon as he cleared Customs he called Samira. She was glad to hear from him. She was at the airport circling and waiting for his call. He told her where he was and then he waited for a well broken-in red Toyota to appear.

As he waited he noticed the same beautiful smiling sun that he saw in London days earlier had now found its way to Detroit and he thought; what a small world. As soon as he saw the Toyota he waved like the propeller on one of Northwest Airlines' turbo props. He realized that his sister had seen him as she immediately slowed and started working her way towards the curb. Once she got there, she hopped out and gave Jamil a big hug.

"Great to have you back, you look great!" she blurted out.

"Great to be home," he quickly responded.

As she pulled away from the airport and onto I-94 she continued, "Mom will have dinner ready by the time we arrive home. I know you are anxious to talk to her about who your mother really is, but I am sure she will want to have dinner first."

"Over the past months I have given it a lot of thought and I have narrowed the possibilities. But it has to be something complex or strange or mom would most likely told me in the email. Now I'm curious as to what was holding back mom from just telling me."

"Me, too." was all Samira could manage as she pulled off I-94 nearing home.

Jamil changed the subject, "What are you going to do for the summer?"

"Working for Mr. Haddad," came the bored reply. She continued, "He says he would like you to work for him also if you want to since his son won't be working there this summer."

As they pulled in the driveway Fatima ran out to greet them. "Good to see you. I have missed you so much! You look great, dorm food must not be so bad after all. Come in, come in. I have dinner ready."

"Told you."

"Mom, please just take a minute before dinner and tell me what the situation is."

"No, it is not that simple."

"Yes, it is. If I am the lawyer's son, fine. If I am adopted, fine. I just want to know, you can provide the details later. And it really does not make any difference to me; you are my mother. Regardless of how you got me, you have taken great care of me for which I am most grateful. I love you. Had the blood tests not uncovered this, I would never have known; you always took care of me as if I really was yours."

"Thanks, you are a good son. That's what I wanted to do, but let's wait. Please sit down, the sooner you eat, the sooner we can have our discussion."

Samira enthusiastically volunteered, "Mom has made some of your favorite things, hummus, falafel, fattoush and mansaf."

"OK, Mom. Dinner is done and the dishes are in the sink."

"Samira you should stay and hear this so you will know everything also. My husband and I had wanted a small family; maybe two, maybe three children. For years we tried and tried to have a family, but I could not become pregnant. I even went to see a gynecologist which was difficult to do because there were very few in Palestine years ago and I had to travel a great distance. After a most thorough exam at a fertility clinic, the doctor said he thought I was not able to become pregnant because of some problem with my tubes. He said it was possible to correct in some cases but it required complex surgery. The facilities were not available where we lived and, in addition, we could not afford it. We did not have any type of health insurance as we know it now. After much discussion, we decided to adopt a child. We went to the local Arab adoption agency and did all the paperwork and waited and waited and waited. Finally, we received a letter saying they had a child for us; a baby boy."

"That was me, I was adopted?"

"Yes."

"Mom, why didn't you tell me before?"

"Was I adopted also?"

"Not so fast, Samira. No, you were not adopted. After Jamil was adopted, I surprisingly became pregnant and you were born. Believe me, becoming pregnant after what I was told was a very big surprise; a very pleasant big surprise."

"Mom, please answer my question. Why didn't you tell me before?"

"Because it is not quite that simple."

"What do you mean, it is not that simple? I was adopted and I am not the lawyer's son. I am really surprised, but can live with that."

"No, you are not the lawyer's son. We thought of taking him in but the lawyer had a sister who took her nephew in."

"So what is not so simple?"

"When we received the letter from the adoption agency to come for you, we expected them to provide some information about the baby. Many of the adoptions in Palestine, and in Israel too at that time, were because the parents were killed and there was no other family member to take the child. If there are family members they usually take other family member's children into their own families. In your case they told us they did not have any idea of who was your family. What happened was that a shooting occurred when Israeli soldiers tried to arrest two Arabs in a market place. The shooting started when a number of Arabs fought back and opened fire on the Israeli soldiers. The adoption agency did not know much about the shooting except it also included a few grenades and a lot... about ten people were killed."

"Mom, please go to the point, what is not so simple. I don't want to learn about the adoption process."

"Be patient, I am getting there. Besides you need to know this detail to understand what happened."

"What happened?"

"The adoption agency told me that those who were not injured walked away, the police removed the dead and the Arab ambulances took the injured to the Arab hospital. At that point there was an infant lying on the ground and no adult claiming it. They could not let it lie there so they took the baby to the same Arab hospital to hold for a day or two until someone claimed it. No one did. So the infant was transferred to the adoption agency, which then wrote to us. We were very pleased to receive you, even without knowing who your parents were."

"I still don't understand. What's the big deal? So what if you don't know who my parents were?"

"You will, and it will answer your other questions. The adoption agency kept checking the people who were killed and injured to see if they had any very young male infants. Because the people running the adoption agency were volunteers and funds were very limited they didn't have much time to check. But after almost three years by process of elimination, the agency found a woman who they believed to be your mother; she was one of those killed that day. They tested a sample of your blood and some of her tissue using the same method used to determine paternity. She was found to be your mother; she was identified as Khadijah and her husband was Uthman Pachachi ..."

"That's a Sunni name!"

"Yes, and you are Omar Pachachi their son."

"NO, no, no, no, it can't be! That's crazy! It can't be me. I'm not a Sunni Muslim, I am a Shiite."

"It was you. Omar Pachachi quickly morphed into Jamil Mansour."

"No, no, no, no! I don't believe it. That's insane! How could an Arab adoption agency give a Sunni child to a Shiite family? Certainly an Arab adoption agency was well aware of the important differences between Sunni and Shiite and the problem this would cause."

"Recall, at the beginning they did not know who you were. It was unlikely that someone in the Shiite Arab marketplace could be a Sunni. Sunnis occasionally did shop there, but it was a rare happening. Three years later when the agency figured out who you were they were embarrassed by

The Answer

the mistake and did not want to let the authorities know that this error had occurred. So they decided to not say anything; I certainly did not want to do anything to disrupt our relationship and the relationship you were developing with Samira. I did some checking on my own and found out your father, Uthman Pachachi, was a baker on the Sunni side of town. I have no idea of why his wife and you were on the Shiite side of town when the shooting started. My husband and I did not want to deal with someone who had a major business and who was well established in the Sunni community."

"Why didn't you ever tell me?"

"There was no need to. If your biology professor had not done some fancy blood test, you would never have known. From what I have been able to learn, the reason the professor indicated you were a hybrid is that your dad apparently was a non-Arab European Christian, probably a British soldier who stayed after British relinquished possession, who converted to Islam, took an Islamic name and then married your mother who was an Arab Muslim."

"No, this can't be. It means I actually am a Sunni Muslim who believes as practices as a Shiite. Oops, and I have said some pretty ugly things about Sunnis!"

Jamil was thinking and talking at the same time. He kept repeating, "I am a Shiite Muslim," until all of a sudden he stopped. He looked at his mother, then at Samira, then back at his mother. "I just recalled, maybe being born as a Sunni, being raised as a Shiite to practice Shiite Islam may not be so strange. Cardinal Jean-Marie Lustiger was born to a Jewish family. To protect him during the Nazi hunt for Jews, his parents gave him to a Catholic family to protect. His mother was one of thousands of French Jews deported to German concentration camps during World War II. She died at the camp in Auschwitz, Poland. Lustiger converted to Catholicism at age 14 before joining the priesthood and eventually becoming a cardinal in the Catholic Church. I guess if a Jew can become a cardinal, a Sunni can become a Shiite."

He continued, "What do I do now? It should not change anything. While I was born to Sunni parents, I have been raised and believe as a Shiite. At least I was born into Islam. It could have been worse, they could have been Christian or a Jew.

The only ones that know are the three of us. The professor just knew that Samira and I were not brother and sister, but he knows nothing of this craziness. Since no one else knows, nothing should change."

"You are not quite correct that we are the only ones who know."

"What do you mean, not the only ones? Who else knows?"

שלושים

THE HOW AND WHY

Jenny and Jacob walked back to the car in shocked silence. Both were deep in their own thoughts which kept flashing through their minds like lightning in a gigantic electrical storm.

As Jenny walked, she kept thinking if Jacob was adopted, I probably am also. But why? And why didn't mom tell us? When I was young, I remember Jacob being there from day one, hence she must have adopted us when we were very young. Is Jacob really my brother?

As Jacob walked alongside of Jenny, he thought, I could have been adopted. In Israel in the 1980s, there was no formal adoption process, people just took in the kids who had lost both parents and had no relatives to look after them. The Rabbis even helped find adults to take in parentless children. Dr. Cohen said Jenny and I have different blood types. We could not be brother and sister, we could not have been adopted from the same family.

Jacob reflected, Mom is the type of person who would take in someone else's kids if the parents were killed or could not take care of the children. Mom said she lived outside of a kibbutz. Maybe some kids in the kibbutz had lost both parents and mom took me or both of us in. But if that happened, why wouldn't she have told us? Who were my parents? Jenny and I can't be brother and sister. Maybe she adopted both of us from different families? Maybe I... or both of us are parentless children who tragically resulted from war and mom took us in. It probably does not make any difference anyway, mom will always be mom to me and Jenny will always be my sister.

Jacob realized that Sarah had kept her secret for two decades. As he got closer to home, the sense of anticipation grew. It was like opening a Chanukah present where you have a pretty good idea it is a shirt but you don't know what kind of shirt.

Even though a myriad of thoughts raced through both their heads like race cars at the Indy 500, they didn't know what to say and rode home buried in their own thoughts which kept looping like an out of control computer program.

By the time they got home, Sarah was there with dinner ready. She knew that both wanted an explanation and dinner could wait. As soon as Jacob pulled the 1988 blue Chevy Nova into the driveway, he and Jenny ran into the house.

"Mother!"

Sarah, replied, "I am here. Yes, I know both of you are anxious to hear what I have to say. Dinner can wait. Please sit down."

"Jenny, please stay - I don't think I could go through this twice. Please, both of you sit down. For years my husband and I lived in the same place and had a wide variety of neighbors and friends—most were Israeli-Jews but some were Arab-Christians and a few Arab-Muslims. We, the workers, and people on the street, got along more than just civilly; we actually got along quite well. But every so often there were military operations of the Palestinians and Israelis fighting each other. We never knew what started it or the extent of the fighting or how long it would last and we were not involved; we just hid and ducked our heads to stay out of the war. When fighting occurred we lived it minute by minute because it went on right around us. Some times it was only a few hours; some times it could go on for days."

"Mom, I don't want a history lesson of the Middle East fighting; what is the answer? How is it that I am not your son?"

"I have always regarded you, and treated you as my very own son."

"But, the blood tests show...."

"I know, let me explain."

"In the early evening one night in March of 1981, large-scale fighting occurred. We did not know who started it; it really did not make any difference to us. It could have been Palestinian rockets or the Israeli military taking some action. But it quickly scaled up to a major fight. Every so often we would hear a rocket go off which seemed like the Palestinians either trying to shoot down the Israeli planes or were shooting rockets into Israel to retaliate, I don't know. It was mass confusion."

"Usually I just found," Sarah explained, "a place in the apartment and hid on the floor in the corner to avoid bullets and bomb fragments. I went to my usual hiding place. The explosions seemed louder and bigger than other times; I think it was just that they were closer. Our electric power went out... then something must have hit a water main or fire hydrant because all of a sudden I could hear water gushing outside. I grabbed my pillow and stayed close to the floor. I was too scared to move; if I left I wouldn't know which way to run. Then my good friend, Elaine, from the next apartment was pounding on my door screaming for me to come out and run. She yelled to me that most of the area we were in was on fire. My husband was at work and I was concerned that if I left and he came home he would not know what happened to me. I had no idea of what to do; I realized that it was best not to stay where I could be trapped by fire, so I got up and ran. Everyone in the street was running to the west; I didn't know why but I followed. I could not keep up with Elaine. We seemed to be running away from the fighting. I recognized some people from the apartments and some from town; there were even some Arabs running the same way to avoid the fighting. It was raining lightly."

"Mom!"

"Be patient. I didn't know where the center of the fighting was, but we must not have been far from it. Bullets were striking the buildings, cars in the street and everything around us. Every so often there was a large explosion like a bomb or grenade. We were running without knowing where we were going; just trying to run away from the fighting, but no one knew for sure where the fighting was or in which direction it was moving."

"Then the rain increased to a steady downpour and I was getting soaked. I could see people running mostly to the west, but a few tired and looked for places to hide safely as most of us kept moving. While we were running a big explosion hit about 50 meters in front of me. I could tell by the way they were running that a couple of people of ahead of me apparently were hit by fragments of that explosion. Two dropped and I was pretty sure they were dead; others screamed in pain from being hit and I received a small nick on my left arm. It ripped through my clothes and I could see blood beginning to come from the area of pain. I stopped, afraid maybe I was running into the war zone instead of away from it. At that instant something exploded just behind me. The person closest to it dropped immediately and two others to my right were probably hit by something as they screamed, stopped running and fell; one grabbed his stomach area and the other, his leg."

"I began to panic as I didn't know whether to continue to run or look for a place of shelter. There were about eight or ten of us still running and we all swerved instantly to the left to avoid the area in front of us. It took us down a small street which was dimly lit. A couple of people in front of me seemed to know their way and they pointed to each other to what was left of a building on our left. It was covered and offered protection from not only the flying debris but also the rain. Everyone by instinct seemed to move to the far wall and lay down to rest. I was exhausted — if not for this refuge, I don't know how much farther I could have gone. The blood from my left arm seemed to have stopped and the area now was numb. I must have fallen asleep almost instantly from exhaustion. When I awoke in the morning, I was freezing from being soaked in the cold but quickly recalled the evening before and how I got to wherever it was that I was!"

"Mom, tell me, I don't need to know all this detail!"

"Here is the answer to your question. While I was trying to quickly think of what to do about being so cold, I heard a baby cry. The sound came from just behind me. I quickly turned over and in doing so realized that everyone there the night before had left except the baby next to me and its mother who was next to it. The infant was sandwiched between us. Apparently the baby's mother was so tired she did not hear it cry so I reached over to awaken her. I shook her lightly and she did not respond. So I shook her a little harder and quickly realized that she was dead. Her clothing was soaked in blood. Apparently she knew she probably would not make it through the night and put the infant down between us ... right up against me. I was shocked; I didn't know what to do."

"That's me?"

"Yes. I knew I couldn't leave you alone there but I did not know what to do with you. After hearing the shelling the night before, the absolute morning silence, except for your crying, seemed strange. I looked around. I did not see anyone alive; everyone else who slept there that night had left. There was rubble, blood, glass, body parts, bodies and ruin everywhere. The area and place were not familiar to me."

"I kept thinking, my husband must be wondering what happened to me; I needed to go home. To go home I figured the best way to find my place was by reversing the way I had come, if I could. So I picked you up. Your blanket was soaking, you were wet and cold and most likely hungry all of which explained your crying. I had nothing to feed you. The place did not look like a war zone; it was a war zone. I saw all the bodies and couldn't help crying for them and for the thought that it could easily have been me."

"Finally after about a half hour of walking and carrying you, I found my place. Other than the water damage all over the floor, things were not too bad. I put you down and unwrapped your soaking blanket. You were soaking because you had not been changed all night. You needed something dry so I decided to wrap you in one of my towels. As I unwrapped the blanket from around you a small pouch fell to the ground. I opened it hoping to find out who you were. It must have served as your mother's purse; it contained her papers, some money and a picture of you with your name. Your mother probably realizing that she was dying wanted whoever found you to know who you were. You are Sharif Rahman. Your mother...."

"Sharif Rahman! Sharif Rahman! That's an Arab name! No! No! This can't be right. Sharif Rahman is an Arab Muslim name. No! No!"

"Yes. Your mother was Halimah Rahman. I later found out your dad was Dr. Amir Rahman and they were Muslims."

"NO, it can't be! It can't be me. I'm not an Arab, a Palestinian, a Muslim. I am an Israeli and Jewish. You always told me I am an Israeli and to be proud of it."

"Yes, that is the way I raised you. I never thought you would find out about not really being my birth son."

"This makes no sense. I speak Hebrew, I was Bar Mitzvah, I have conducted Sabbath services, I fast on Yom Kippur. How did the rabbi permit me to become Bar Mitzvah if I am not Jewish? Did you take me through a mikvah conversion ceremony?"

"All good questions. When I came to the United States everyone believed you were my son and since you could read and speak Hebrew, and not Arabic, everyone assumed you were Jewish. So I never took you through a *mikvah* conversion service because there was no need to, everyone assumed you were Jewish because I your mother was Jewish and you spoke Hebrew as your native language. When it came to Bar Mitzvah time, again everyone including the rabbi assumed you were Jewish. No one ever asked, I just let them assume what they wanted to."

"That means I am not officially a Jew but I have been Bar Mitzvah; that is probably a first! Well I am not a Jew according to the conservative or orthodox but the reform probably consider me a Jew because I have been Bar Mitzvah. So what is it; am I a Jew or not? I guess it depends on whether you ask a reform rabbi or a conservative one. Even though I have been Bar Mitzvah, a conservative rabbi will probably not marry me if he or she knew. This blows my mind. What am I?"

"Jacob, I am sorry. I never thought anyone would find out. To me you are a Jew, that is what you believe and practice. You are a good Jew, you have gone to services regularly and practiced your beliefs."

"Mother, why did you bring this Arab into our household!?"

"Jenny, I know you are only joking but it raises an interesting point. Had Sharif been raised by the Rahmans, he would have grown up speaking Arabic, celebrating Ramadan and believing the Israelis were the source of the Middle East conflict by occupying Palestinian land. However, being raised as Jacob Goodman he speaks Hebrew, celebrates Rosh Hashana and Yom Kippur and believes that the Arabs/Palestinians are the source of the conflict in the Middle East for trying to take Israel from us. So it shows that people believe what they are taught, right or wrong, good or bad. Further, it shows that people's beliefs probably can be changed. It gives me hope for resolution of the Middle East situation."

"My husband knew the Rahman family by word of mouth. He knew that your dad was Amir Rahman, a local area Arab physician, who was also probably dead because his clinic building was one of the many buildings destroyed and probably why he was not running with his wife."

"At the beginning my husband did not want us to keep you. But given the chaotic situation, we did not know where we could safely find any Arabs who would be willing to be responsible for you. He was concerned that the Israelis would find out we had you and then we could be accused of hiding a Palestinian. I understood and shared his concern; it was real. However, I told him we can not turn you over to the authorities because there are some that would want to treat you as any other Arab. He said nothing but stared at me for awhile; then nodded. I was relieved. We realized that if we stayed in our small town someone would quickly find out. We concluded that we had to move to some town where no one knew us in the next day or two. We had paid our rent for the month so the landlord would not chase us."

Sarah went on, "The next day I moved to a small town 20 km north of where we were and where no one knew us. My husband stayed a few days to pack our stuff and then he joined us. Everyone assumed the boy, that's you, was our son. Ever since then you have been my son; Sharif Rahman instantly became Jacob Goodman. The only real problem we had was when I became pregnant with Jenny the doctor seemed to be suspicious that I had not delivered before because I was ignorant of so many things regarding pregnancy and delivery. I got around that by telling him you were my deceased sister's child whom I had taken in."

"Then I really am your daughter?"

"Yes, Jenny. You both are my children."

Jacob interjected, "Why didn't you ever tell me?"

"There was no need to. If Jenny had not developed aplastic anemia, you probably would never have known."

"This is crazy. It means I am a Palestinian Jew?"

"Yes. You were born an Arab whose parents practiced Islam, now you are an Arab practicing Judaism as strange as that may seem!

"That explains why my facial bone scan showed Arab features and why the IDF could not find a birth certificate for me. I hope the IDF doesn't ask questions. What do I do now? It should not change anything. The only ones that know are the three of us. Do I need to notify the IDF that the ethnicity on my application is in error? My religion is correct; just the ethnicity is in error. But that does not make any difference, all the IDF was interested in is that one is a Jew, not where they come from and there are Jews of various ethnic backgrounds."

"You are not quite correct that we are the only ones who know."

"What do you mean, not the only ones? Who else knows?"

"When they diagnosed Jenny's condition as aplastic anemia, the doctors told me that if the transfusions did not work, they would most likely recommend a bone marrow transplant. When I asked could you or I donate to her, they said not always. The doctors told me that they had to test our blood to see if there was a match. Further, that if there is more than one possible match/donor, they prefer the younger one. After I learned they were going to test your blood I knew that you would most likely find out and I would have to tell you everything."

Sarah continued, "In addition, at the time you came into my life, I was sure your dad had been killed when his clinic was destroyed. However, just before we left Israel to come to the states, one day when I was going to the bakery I saw a poster ad on a wall in the market that a Dr. Rahman was reopening his medical clinic. I couldn't believe it was the same Dr. Rahman until I noticed a statement that it was dedicated to his deceased wife and son who had died in an attack. Instantly I realized he had survived the attack. However, by that time I had taken care of you for a number of years and you and Jenny had become so attached I just couldn't turn you over to a man neither you nor I knew and tear you away from Jenny and me."

Sarah paused and then went on, "Your father is somewhere in Israel or Palestine who thought both his wife and son were dead. I knew if I had a child somewhere out in the world who I thought was dead but who was actually alive, I would certainly want to know ... to see him and hug my child again. So weeks ago when I realized that you most likely would find out, I searched the Internet to see if his clinic was there and sure enough I found it. I sent an email to the clinic for Dr. Rahman informing him of the situation and telling them that I wanted to make contact because his son was alive and well.

"At first he thought it was a hoax. He said it did not make sense because if I had his son, why did I wait 20 years to contact him. I was a little ashamed, but I told him even though I did not give birth to you, I regarded you as my son since I raised you for two decades, I came to love you and you had become attached to Jenny, and she to you. Given the turmoil of the Middle East, I thought the stable situation you had here was better for you. He responded with emails asking a number of questions about our area, me, my husband. When I could describe the place in detail, and provide answers to all his questions including many that only people there that night would know, he realized I was who I said I was. What further gave me credibility was that I was not asking anything from anybody. I assured him that I wanted nothing more than to have him know his son was alive. He said his wife's body was recovered from the street but they told him they did not find his son's body. He was sure you were dead because there was no one to protect you that night."

"Mom, forget about him. I don't remember him and he only knew me a very short period of time. It is like we never met. We don't know each other."

"Jacob, I can forget about him; but he cannot forget about you. If the situation were reversed, I would want to meet and know my long-lost child. Some day when you become a parent you will understand."

"Once he realized I was who I said I was, he seemed to happily acknowledge that you could be his son. He can easily verify if you are his son by the blood test used in paternity cases. He thanked me many times over and over for having rescued and taken care of you; he seems truly grateful. He would like to meet you this summer."

"No, I don't want to meet someone I don't know and especially anyone who is an Arab Muslim. Further, I have no time. I will be in the States until 9 August and I have to report to the IDF as soon as I am back."

"He told me he has an older child, a daughter. He offered to have you come and spend the summer with him and his daughter, your sister, who is a year or two older than you. I understand why you can't go because of your commitment to the IDF. He even offered to have Jenny come with you, all at his expense. Further, he offered to pay my way so he could thank me in person. I realize that because of your IDF schedule you will not have time this summer to spend time with him. But, you will be very close to where he lives and practices. I am sure you can find time to meet him sometime. Even if you don't like the man or your sister, you will have met him and in the future not regret not having at least met him. I would like to take him up on his offer. Let's think how we can all meet in Jerusalem. I would like to go back for a visit but you know we don't have the money. This will give me the opportunity to go back and you the opportunity to meet him."

Jenny spoke up. "This is a shock to me too. I had no idea you were an imposter, not my brother and an Arab imposter at that! Further, now you have a 'real' sister!" she said with a teasing smile. "Mom is right for the reasons she gave; you should try and work it in your schedule to meet him when you have some free time. The two of you will geographically be very close to each other. Let's think how to do it."

"I don't know. This is so weird. My whole world has changed. Let me think about it."

Abraham's Tears

Thirty-one
PROBLEM

"John, John."

"Eliz, what's the matter, you sound like you are crying. You are? Why?"

"Yesterday, I think, yes – 1 June, Bob went to the urologist because of the male thing, the urgency and frequency urination problem you males have. In doing the tests they found he has a tumor on the left kidney and will have to have it removed in a day or two. It may not have spread but we don't know at this point. In any event, he will not be able to travel in time for us to use the raffle tickets. We want to give the tickets to you and your family."

"Oh, my. I am so sorry. Poor Bob. How is he handling all this?

"Not well, he is scared it may have spread. But in any event, we want the four of you to have the tickets and take the trip."

"Thank you very much; it is very kind of you. Our prayers are with you."

Abraham's Tears

Zweiundreißig
TRAVEL DETAILS

To: GoldbergAD@gmail.com
From: HBerniseWECB@gmail.com
Subject: Re: Our Meeting
Date: 17 July 00

Dr. Goldberg:

My wife will come with me and we will vacation a little after you and I have completed business.

We arrive on 8 August on Swiss Air #949 at 15:40.

I look forward to meeting you

Hans

Abraham's Tears

ثلاثة وثلاثون

OH, BROTHER

"When you sent me the email last fall, I knew you were on the path to finding out about being adopted and I wanted to tell you everything. Just before I left Palestine for the United States, I became aware that your dad's bakery was still doing a good business in the Sunni section of town, but I knew nothing more about him than that. By then I had raised you for almost five years, you and Samira had become attached and since you did not know, I remained silent. I was probably wrong in doing so, but you had lived with us for three years before we found out who you really were and you had lived with us and Samira longer than you had with your birthparents."

Fatima shared her thinking, "As a parent if I had a child that disappeared, I would always wonder what happened to him/her and if they might be alive, and if so, what kind of life they were leading. And if for some fortunate reason he or she was alive, I would go to the other side of the earth to meet them. So when you made me aware that you knew, I sent some emails to the town city hall asking about the bakery and Uthman Pachachi. I told them about you being Uthman Pachachi's son. At first they thought it an extortion plot. I assured them that I only wanted Uthman meet his son, Omar. I was not asking for anything and only wanted to inform Uthman that his son was alive and well. Finally when they realized I was not asking for anything and had details that only someone who had lived there at that time would be in possession of, they informed me that Uthman died a few years ago. They also informed me that Uthman and his wife had another son, Yazid, who is about five years older than you."

"Mom, forget about him. I don't remember him at all; it is like we never met. We don't know each other."

"Jamil, I can forget about him, but now that he knows you are alive I doubt that he can forget about you. Yazid has sent me a number of emails and he seems very interested in his you; you are his only living relative and he has not yet married. If the situation were reversed, I would want to meet and know my only living relative. He can easily verify if you are his brother by the same blood test your professor used. He thanked me many times over for having taken care of you; he was truly grateful. He would like to meet you."

"No, I don't want to meet someone I don't know and especially someone who is a Sunni. If he knew what I had said about Sunni's, he wouldn't want to meet me!"

"He offered to have you come and spend the summer with him. I can't make you go, but I think you should. As an added incentive, he even offered to have your sister come with you at his expense. Further, he wants me to come so he can thank me. He will even cover my airfare. He owns his dad's bakery but does not work there. He took training and works something like a nurse managing the local medical clinic. By using some sort of charge card for both the bakery and clinic charges, he has accumulated lots of airline miles but can never use them. He wants to use them so the three of us can visit him. I think it best that the two of you go and spend the summer. Even if you do not like your brother, you will at least have met him and in the future not regret not having done so. You and your sister will be able to see a part of the world you that you came from, but do not remember and where I can't afford to send you. There are places I can now go and see because I hold a United States passport where I could not go before. I will meet you in Jerusalem at the end of the summer for a week. I will show you where we used to live. You will be seeing your roots."

Samira spoke up for the first time. "Wow, I am not sure what to say other than Mom is right. You should go and meet him. I will go with you."

"I don't know. This is so weird. I was sure I was the son of the lawyer. My whole world has changed. This morning when I left London I was a Shiite. Now I am told, no that is not correct. Now a few hours later and after flying across the Atlantic I suddenly became a Sunni Muslim!   Let me think about it."

Abraham's Tears

שלושים וארבע
A BUSY SUMMER

On 1 April Jacob flew to Nashville, Tennessee and took a bus to Knoxville to begin his course at the National Forensics Academy.

> To: Dr. Levine@IDF.org
> From: JacobCA@gmail.com
> Subject: Re: Forensic Academy
> Date: 9 April 00
>
> I was not a bone marrow match but my mother was. The procedure went smoothly and my sister is recovering well. She has begun doing day-to-day things but on a very limited basis. I was told that by June 1st she will be as good as new.
>
> My first week went well. They move FAST here and cover a lot of ground; it is an excellent course.
>
> I will keep you updated.
>
> Jacob

> To: Sarah.Goodman@yahoo.com; JennyCA@gmail.com
> From: JacobCA@gmail.com
> Subject: Miss the two of you
> Date: 11 April 00

Things were very hectic the first week, sorry I didn't have a chance to write. There is a lot of interesting stuff here to learn. It will be quite helpful to me.

The area is beautiful. The drive along I-40 from Nashville to Knoxville is very nice, especially now in the spring when everything is blooming.

Jenny, let me know how you are doing.

Love, Jacob

To: JacobCA@gmail.com
From: JennyCA@gmail.com
Subject: Re: Miss the two of you
Date: 13 April 00

Glad you are enjoying your course.

I'm getting stronger each day. I must be better because I asked about the possibility of getting back to soccer and Dr. Cohen just smiled. He said in the fall.

Love, Jenny

To: JennyCA@gmail.com
From: JacobCA@gmail.com
Subject: Re: Miss the two of you
Date: 22 April 00

Last weekend a couple of us went for a ride to Chattanooga. While we in the West have the "Four Corners," here if you do a little bit of climbing at a place near Chattanooga you can see seven different states. Add it to your list of things 'to do,' it's really cool.

How are you doing? I assume you are back in school by now.

Love, Jacob

A Busy Summer

To: JacobCA@gmail.com
From: JennyCA@gmail.com
Subject: Re: Miss the two of you
Date: 27 April 00

Yes I am back in school. I am even doing some things around the house here to help mom. Since I mostly sit, instead of watching TV or surfing the computer, I found a part-time job at the travel agency next door to the high school. I can sit and earn some money!

Mom won a raffle at work to two tickets to see the LA Dodgers. I feel well enough to go.

Love, Jenny

To: Dr. Levine@IDF.org
From: JacobCA@gmail.com
Subject: Re: Forensic Academy
Date: 3 May 00

We are getting a lot of material about DNA testing and evidence. That is a very powerful tool. Most individuals here are interested in DNA evidence for use in a criminal trial. Even though we are usually not interested in criminal prosecutions, with physical (DNA) evidence so small that it is not visible with the eye, one can learn a lot of critically important information that would be useful to us. It will also be helpful in positively identifying targets so we don't error in going after the wrong person.

I'm glad I had a chance to really learn this stuff.

Jacob

To: JacobCA@gmail.com
From: JennyCA@gmail.com

Subject: Improving
Date: 11 May 00

I assume you are busy.

I am improving very quickly; each day is better than the previous one. It is about time to start looking for summer work. I really don't want to go back to In-N-Out Burger. I would be on my feet all day. While I am better, that would probably be too much for me in June. By July I hope to be 100%.

When you have time, let us hear from you.

Love, Jenny

To: JennyCA@gmail.com
From: JacobCA@gmail.com
Subject: Re: Improving
Date: 16 May 00

Sorry you have not heard from me, but not only do we have class eight hours a day; homework is very time consuming. We have complicated problems to solve, and they take a lot of time.

If you like your part-time job, why don't you see if you can stay on in the summer when they have their big travel season?

Say "hello" to Mom for me.

Love, Jacob

To: JacobCA@gmail.com
From: JennyCA@gmail.com
Subject: Re: Improving
Date: 20 May 00

Brother, sometimes you surprise me. Great idea! I did get a summer job at the travel agency and it has some neat perks. We receive discounts on travel, first choice on special deals, etc. I can get you a discount to come home from TN before you go to work in DC this summer. Just let me know the dates you want to travel.

Mom, got some company award. They like her work. For her it is good job security.

Love, Jenny

To: JennyCA@gmail.com
From: JacobCA@gmail.com
Subject: Re: Improving
Date: 27 May 00

Thanks sis! I can fly BNA ? LAX on June 16th. I need to be in DC June 30th.

I am looking forward to being home with you and Mom.

Love, Jacob

To: JacobCA@gmail.com
From: JennyCA@gmail.com
Subject: Re: Improving
Date: 2 June 00

You're all set to come home on the 16th, see the attached schedule which gives flight numbers and times. In addition, I found out that most of the first-class seats have not been sold so I was able to put you on a waiting list. If they don't sell them all, they probably will move you to first class and then sell your seat again!

Talk about perks! There is a student group going to Europe on July 15th. Because I work here, I can get the tour at cost. In addition, they needed chaperones and mom is going for free because she will be a chaperone; she can use her vacation time. We see the

UK, France, Belgium and Germany. The tour ends in Berlin on July 31st.

Rather than come home on July 31st mom had the idea of going on to see Dr. Rahman. He is happy to pay for the ticket because it is much cheaper than her coming from the United States.

We were planning to fly to Ben Gurion International Airport from Berlin but Dr. Rahman said for him to cross into Israel and then all of us cross to the West Bank probably is not worth the hassle. I think we will fly to Amman directly on July 31st. I am going to stay with Dr. Rahman's daughter and mom with one of his sisters. For you the "honored one," Dr. Rahman will take the day and put up with the hassle of the crossing. We will pick you up at TLV on 9 August! This is working out great!!!

I am looking forward to seeing you on June 16th. We can finalize our plans then.

Love, Jenny

To: JennyCA@gmail.com
From: JacobCA@gmail.com
Subject: Re: Improving
Date: 5 June 00

It sounds great for you and mom. I guess I will meet Dr. Rahman and my "sister" after all.

Even though you really are not my sister and I have a "real" sister, I want you to know that I still and always will regard you as my one real sister.

One small correction regarding your plans. The IDF has booked me to travel TLV to Jerusalem by bus on the 9th. I better follow their desires so meet me at the bus station in Jerusalem on the 9th at 20:50. I will be on Bus #81 from the airport.

Love, Jacob

Abraham's Tears

Thirty-five
PLANNING HOLY LAND TRIP

"Eliz, you asked about our schedule. We need to be in Jerusalem on August 9th. Therefore, we will leave Sydney on August 8th because of next day arrival. The brochure says there is a very convenient bus, Bus #81 which connects with our flight. If we take that bus, our hotel is just one block from the bus station in Jerusalem. Bus 81 leaves the airport at 20:00 and gets us to the Jerusalem bus stop at about 20:50. We return here on August 23rd. Let's get together right after that so we can tell you about what we experienced."

"How is Bob doing?

Abraham's Tears

Sechsunddreißig
FLIGHT CANCELED

To: GoldbergAD@gmail.com
From: HBerniseWECB@gmail.com
Subject: Re: Our Meeting
Date: 8 August 00

Dr. Goldberg:

Our flight today was canceled because of mechanical problems. The earliest they can rescheduled me is tomorrow the 9th but I will not arrive until about 18:30.

There is only one seat on that flight so my wife will have to come on the 10th.

Hans

Abraham's Tears

ثلاثون و سبعة

MEETING FAMILY

As their flight lifted off from Detroit, Samira jokingly teased Jamil, "This is a great deal—you get a brother and I get a free trip abroad."

Jamil quickly jumped on her, "Cut it out. The only reason I am going is that I have no job for the summer and this is a free trip to where we are from but don't remember. It is a great opportunity because Mom promised to meet us at the end of the summer in Jerusalem and she will take us to the places where we lived when we were young. I know she has thought of going back for a visit but never thought she could afford it. This works out great for all of us. Win-Win."

Jamil put his seat back to think. It all seemed like a bad dream that would not end.

As El Al flight 12 approached Ben Gurion International Airport near Tel Aviv, Samira looked out intently. This was her first real trip out of the United States. To her Canada was just across the bridge and she did not consider it a foreign country. She was excited now. Also, this was the area of the world where she was born and her mother had lived much of her life. Given what Jamil had learned about the Middle East while in London, he expected

Israeli security to be tight at the airport and elsewhere. However, it was much more thorough than he expected. Finally he and Samira had cleared immigration and customs. After all what do two poor college students have to declare! As they came out of the door, he saw an older gentleman holding a sign in English that read "Jamil and Samira." Jamil walked over, introduced himself and asked, "Do you speak English?"

"Of course. I am Bakr and will be your driver," came the reply. "Are these all of your bags?"

"Yes," Jamil responded.

Both Jamil and Samira left the driving to Bakr and were awed by the surroundings and especially the languages. They recognized Arabic and English, but most people spoke Hebrew. Many signs contained all three languages.

The car pulled to a stop in a parking lot of a building which Jamil recognized as a medical clinic. Jamil asked, "What are we doing here?" Bakr answered, "You claim to be Yazid's brother. He would like you to take a blood test to make sure. Please, come." They followed the driver to a blood lab. When they arrived there, there was an individual in his robes getting his blood drawn. The driver turned to Samira and stated, "The blood lab would like to have a sample of your blood to run as a control. It should show no relationship to Jamil. Is that ok with you?"

She looked at Jamil, shrugged and answered, "Sure, why not."

As the Arab who just had his blood drawn was getting up to leave, Jamil rose to go over to the designated chair to have his blood drawn. Before he got there, the person leaving the blood draw chair came up to him and asked, "Are you Jamil Mansour?"

"Yes, how did you know?"

"I am Yazid and was here having my blood drawn for the comparison."

Jamil stood there absolutely speechless. He did not know what to say or do. How could this Arab in his robes be his brother? But only his brother would have known he was in Israel and at this medical clinic.

"Hi," came his very weak voice. "I... I...." Since he could not speak, Jamil slowly reached out his hand to the hand that had been extended to him and shook it in a respectful greeting.

"I know this must be as much a surprise to you, as it is to me. I was sure you were killed in the gun fight when our mother was killed."

'... our mother ...' the thought shot thru Jamil. That was correct, Yazid's mother was his biological mother, even though he had always regarded Fatima as his mother.

"I had no idea what you or your sister would look like. The last time I saw you, you were only a few months old. As soon as your blood is drawn the four of us can leave. We have a lot of catching up to do." He turned to Samira, smiled and said, "Welcome – it is nice to know I have a sister!"

Samira wasn't sure what to do or say. Even after finding out Jamil had a brother, she had not thought of Yazid as a brother. She stood up and said, "Nice to meet you."

Jamil asked, "Do you know when the results of these blood tests will be back?"

Yazid gave an I don't know shrug and looked at the nurse, "Probably two or three days." she replied.

After leaving the hospital, Jamil asked his Yazid where they were going. His brother informed Jamil and Samira that they were headed to have dinner and over dinner he would explain where they would be staying, what they would be doing, etc over the next few weeks.

At dinner Yazid continued, "Let me explain what I have in mind for the next couple of weeks. We can modify it to suit your desires to some extent, but to a great extent it is dictated by the logistics of the difficult and time consuming crossing from the West Bank area to Israel, and back, the much better living conditions are in Israel, and the fact that your mother will take you to much of the West Bank area when she is here. Because of the great difference in living conditions even though my main medical clinic is in Arab territory, I started a wholesale medical distribution business in Israel just so I would have good reason to come to Israel and make it easier to get through the check points. In addition, the building I rented has an apartment on the second floor so I can stay on either side of the border for days at a time without having to cross back and forth, which Israel makes a real hassle. Also, it is easier for me to get supplies shipped here, and then personally take them across the border to my clinic. By establishing a business here I have made friends here, both Arab and Israeli, which makes my life easier and offers many more opportunities. It helps because some here want to do business on the Arab side and I have the contacts there, so I have worked myself to a good spot."

Yazid continued, "I think the most important thing, regarding on which side of the border you spend your time and what you see and do now is dictated by the fact that your mother will be here. She can take and show you the Arab West Bank far better than she can show you Israel. At the same time, I can show you Israel much better than she can. So I worked out with an Israeli business acquaintance that for the next month you will be staying at a kibbutz called Neve Shalom where he lives. It is located midway between Jerusalem and Tel Aviv about 20 km from Ben Gurion Airport. I thought it would be a good experience for the two of you because the Jewish-Arab village of Neve Shalom/Wahat Al-Salam, is a place where Arabs and Israelis co-exist in peace. It is a place which the Israelis claim fulfills the teachings of the 133rd Psalm, "How good and pleasant it is for everyone to live in unity."

Jamil interjected, "You said, midway between Jerusalem and Tel Aviv and 20 km from the airport means the country is only about 40 km wide?"

Yazid replied, "Yes. Israel is only about the size of New Jersey and a lot smaller than Michigan.

"Wow, that is small." Samira responded. "In listening to the news about the Middle East and Israel, I somehow had thought that Israel was the size of Germany, France, Spain or larger."

Yazid continued, "During the week I often spend a night or two in the apartment above my wholesale business. However, I spend a lot of my time on the other side of the border because of my position in the clinic in the West Bank and the bakery which I still manage. On the weekends I will stay here in Israel so we can travel and visit the interesting and historic places. Since we will be in Israel on the weekend, we need to remember the Jewish Sabbath starts at sundown on Friday and goes to sundown on Saturday. Most things begin to wind down on Friday afternoon in preparation for the Sabbath. That has been their custom for over five thousand years. However, non-Jewish and less religious Jews still have business open and we can travel without too much problem."

As they pulled in the driveway of Neve Shalom, a young man came up to greet them. Yazid made the introductions, "Jamil meet Douglas, the business man I told you about. Douglas meet Jamil, my brother, and his sister, Samira. Unfortunately, here in Israel space is very limited and everyone needs to share a room. Jamil you will be staying with Douglas and Samira you will be staying with a young woman, Michelle, from Paris who attends UCLA during the school year."

> To: Fatima.Mansour@yahoo.com
> From: JamilM@gmail.com
> Subject: Hello from half-way around
>   the world!
> Date: 27 June 2000
>
>> I'm glad I came. Israel is an interesting place. Yazid is nice but very busy between his medical clinic and bakery in the West Bank and a wholesale medical supply business in Israel. Since you can show us around the West Bank area and you are not familiar with Israel, he will show us Israel and let you show us the West Bank. He also knows you would prefer not to be in Israel. We will be staying at staying at a kibbutz called Neve Shalom which is located midway between Jerusalem and Tel Aviv. By staying in Israel we will not have to go thru the hassle of crossing the border daily. Many Arab workers do cross daily and it is a big problem taking lots of time. He has an apartment above his wholesale business in Jerusalem which permits him to stay on whatever side of the border

he desires. He will work during the week and joins us for the weekend. It is more fun when we travel and sightsee on the weekends. He doesn't seem like a brother, while Samira who is not my real sister seems like a sister. Well... I think you understand.

Hope you are having some fun this summer.

Say "hello" to Charlie for me.

Your "son", Jamil

To: JamilM@gmail.com
From: Fatima.Mansour@yahoo.com
Subject: Hello from half-way around the world!
Date: 3 July 2000

I'm fine and glad you are pleased at making the decision to go. Take your time to get to know Yazid. Remember you have known Samira for about two decades. Yes, see Israel now as I don't want to be there more than I have to. I no longer have a husband because of the Israelis.

Love, Mom

That weekend at lunch, Yazid told Jamil that the results of the blood tests had come back from the hospital. He was in fact Omar and they were indeed brothers. Scientifically, there was no question. Jamil's mother was correct. Yazid extended his hand, "Hello brother." Jamil extended his hand, "Hello brother."

To: Fatima.Mansour@yahoo.com
From: JamilM@gmail.com
Subject: We are traveling some
Date: 15 July 2000

The blood results came back and confirmed that I am Yazid's brother.

Samira and I have been to Tel Aviv, much of Jerusalem and the Dead Sea which is where the angel Gabriel came.

I am having trouble understanding this country. Abdel Rahman Zuabi, an Arab, was a temporary Justice for nine months on the Israel Supreme Court.[1] I can't imagine any Israeli ever being on any court or in any important position in any Arab country.

We are getting along fine. Because the kibbutz is in an Arab-Israeli city, I can get to the mosque and no one here seems to care. To me it is strange that the Jews only pray morning and evening and not five times a day. Oh well, they do their thing, I do mine. No one has said anything to me about my going to the mosque, I think they understand. I did sit in on one of their Sabbath services just to observe and learn; very different. It was apparent that Abraham is the father to both Islam and Judaism.

Samira and I are looking forward to your coming. Do you know your arrival date yet?

Your "son", Jamil

To: JamilM@gmail.com
From: Fatima.Mansour@yahoo.com
Subject: Re: We are traveling some
Date: 22 July 2000

Yes, there are plenty of ritualistic differences between Islam and Judaism. However, the ritualistic differences

---

[1]. Another Arab, Salim Joubran, was a permanent Justice on the Israel Supreme Court but that did not take place until after the timeline of this novel.

are not very important. What is important are the differences or similarities as to how one should live their life. I know your militant friends do not believe this, but I think there are more similarities than differences as to how one should live their life in relating to others. If followed, I believe each will produce a good, kind, understanding person who will treat others as they want to be treated. With religion, the critical issue I have learned is do your own thing, just don't try and impose it on others. The problems arise when one religion tries to impose its tenants on those of another religion. So much for philosophy of religion 101!

I am trying to finalize my work schedule. Originally I was going to fly the same route you did. If I did you would need to pick me up at Ben Gurion airport. However, I found a tour operator that had a number of empty seats they were desperately trying to sell. So I worked a deal where I get air and bus for the same number of miles as just the air with the other tour operator. More later.

Love, Mom

To: Fatima.Mansour@yahoo.com
From: JamilM@gmail.com
Subject: More traveling
Date: 28 July 2000

This time we went to the Weitzmann Institute at Rehov. Wow, what a really modern technology and innovation center. I was amazed to find this in the desert and in Israel. I always heard Jews were in business and banking; I never expected to see them at the cutting edge of technology. I was wrong!

On the tour they told us that much of the technology used today such as the cell phone (invented by Motorola, with its largest R&D center in Israel), most of the Windows NT operating system, voice mail technology, VOIP technology, instant messaging (ICQ), firewall security software, Intel wireless computer chips, numerous medicines, and miniature video camera capsules to examine internal organs all were invented in Israel. It seemed self serving. If I had not been here for a number of weeks I doubt that I would believe it, but I think it is probably true.

What surprises me is that no one seems to be actively discussing attacking the Arabs. On the other hand, if they were, they probably would not make it public. The concern that most seem to have is a worry about suicide bombers or some rockets that are shot into the southern part of the country. We have not heard of any suicide bombers since we have been here. Yazid does not worry about it; he has figures which indicate more people die/100,000 in Detroit from gun fire than in Israel.

I miss you and am looking forward to our travels to where Samira and I grew up.

What are you going to do with Charlie when you come here?

Your "son", Jamil

To: JamilM@gmail.com
From: Fatima.Mansour@yahoo.com
Subject: Re: More traveling
Date: 4 Aug 2000

I have heard of the Weitzmann Institute but I thought it was the usual propaganda. You seem to have been impressed with it which is rare. Not much impresses you.

I just found out I arrive on 9 Aug at 17:15. Our bus is scheduled to get us to Jerusalem at 22:50. The bus number is 81. I will meet you at the bus depot in Jerusalem at about 22:50.

Charlie is going to "visit" at the neighbors who have two cats.

I can't wait to see the two of you, meet Yazid and see "home" again.

Love, Mom

To: Fatima.Mansour@yahoo.com
From: JamilM@gmail.com
Subject: Aug 9th
Date: 6 Aug 2000

> We will be at the bus station on 9 August at 22:50 to pick you up.
>
> Yazid has told me a number of times how thankful he is for what you did; now he has a brother! I am pretty sure he is planning to reward you in some way for what you did, but I don't know how. I too am most appreciative of what you did. If you hadn't, I wouldn't be here. He has not asked whether I practice Sunni or Shiite and I have not volunteered. I think he suspects our family is Shiite and he is 100% Sunni. It is probably best not to discuss any of this with him until we know each other better. My guess at this time is that it will not be a big issue with him.
>
> Samira sends "hello." I know she is anxious to see you and get started on our trip with you.
>
> With love, your son, Jamil

Even thought they were in a very interesting country, while waiting for "mother," the days waiting seemed to drag for both Jamil and Samira. Over the summer he had gotten to know Yazid quite well. He felt very comfortable around him and sensed a growing friendship developing. It wasn't the immediate sense of the growing closer that concerned Jamil; it was where it would lead. Would he ever feel towards "his brother" as he did towards Fatima who wasn't his birth mother, but the woman who saved, raised and cared for him. Samira was not his true sister yet he felt closer to her. He kept telling himself, don't worry about it, it would take its own course. Just let things go day-to-day and see what happens. He was relieved that Yazid seemed very relaxed about the issue and also willing to take it day-by-day.

Finally the 9th came and Yazid told Jamil, "I have to work until about 19:00. I will then come here, pick up the two of you and we can go to dinner at a pizza place in Jerusalem which is not far from the bus depot. After dinner it will be just a 10 minute or so walk to the bus station."

"Sounds great." responded Jamil.

As evening came on, the three of them got ready. Jamil and Samira packed up their stuff as they would stay that night in Jerusalem with their mother and then join her on a trip to where they were born and lived as children.

Yazid had a jeep-like vehicle so there was sufficient room for the four of them plus Jamil's and Samira's luggage. By the time they got to the restaurant, all were hungry. The menu was in Hebrew, Arabic and English so Jamil and Samira could read it in two languages. But they did not recognize most of the items. They quickly realized that because it was a kosher restaurant they could not have meat on the pizza. They decided to order one medium cheese and one large vegetable one and share.

They finished dinner and were enjoying sherbet for dessert when Yazid looked at his watch. "It is about 22:25 so we should leave soon to be there on time. This will give us time to walk to the bus station before 22:50."

A few minutes later they got up and Yazid went over to pay the bill. As Yazid was paying the bill they were all startled by a very large and loud explosion not too far away. Samira jumped with fright and grabbed Jamil. Jamil had no idea of what it was and quickly looked to Yazid. Yazid, turned and quickly said, "Stay put. Let's see if there is another or there is gun fire. It may just be a car bomb."

One minute. Two minutes.

"It seems like an isolated car bomb. We have plenty of time to walk to the bus station. The explosion seems to have come from that direction and we can see what happened."

Jamil quickly looked at his watch, 22:32. He thought about fifteen minutes before bus 81 was to arrive.

Jamil and Samira followed Yazid out the door and down the street toward the bus station. As they walked they turned north out of the restaurant, they saw smoke rising from the area of the bus station in the distance. Yazid offered, "Looks like a car bomb."

Jamil was relieved that Yazid thought it was a car bomb and his mother's bus did not arrive for another 10 more minutes.

Abraham's Tears

שלושים ושמונה

MEETING DAD

As Jacob's flight descended into Washington National Airport, he looked out intently as he had never been to the DC area before and wanted to see all the historical landmarks. He was a particular fan of Thomas Jefferson and wanted to see the Jefferson Memorial from the air.

When he made it to his room, he unpacked and powered up his laptop. There was one message.

> To: JacobCA@gmail.com
> From: Dr. Levine@IDF.org
> Subject: Your Vacation
> Date: 30 June 00
>
>> Please recall the important things you were taught.
>>
>> Enjoy your vacation.
>>
>> Dr. Levine

Jacob smiled; he recalled that his communications would be monitored.

To: JennyCA@gmail.com
From: JacobCA@gmail.com
Subject: Your Travels
Date: 12 July 00

I am enjoying my work.

I hope you and mom are enjoying Europe. We can celebrate your getting well when we are all together. I am looking forward to it and meeting everyone.

Love, Jacob

To: JacobCA@gmail.com
From: JennyCA@gmail.com
Subject: Wow! What a surprise
Date: 2 August 00

We arrived here 31 July and were met by Dr. Amir Rahman and your sister, Rashida Rahman. They are very nice and we can communicate reasonably well since their English is pretty good and they know some Hebrew. So between English and a little Hebrew we get by.

I am not sure how to describe this place other than if I was here I would try and get out as soon as I could with all the effort I could muster. Our situation here is better than most for two reasons. First, Dr. Rahman's income as a physician is much better than most Arabs and second, hospitality seems central to Palestinian culture and after all, you could say we are "family".

There is income inequality here like anywhere else. A few even have swimming pools but most live in poverty spelled with a capital P. Generally, there is not much running water and the electricity does not work all the time so it's difficult to refrigerate food. Further, there is not much food, especially fruit and meat. It makes even many of LA's poor areas look very upscale.

Besides the physical hardships, those who travel to Israel to work have an awful time; it can take hours to cross the border. It is not like going from Seattle to Vancouver or from San Diego to Tijuana. I know it is for security reasons, it just seems very, very, very slow, but I don't understand all the security implications. So don't expect much; this is subsistence-level living. More later, I have to go.

Mom and I hope to go shopping in Israel for food later today. I am really looking forward to being in Israel and hope we can get to Jerusalem.

Love, Jenny

To: JennyCA@gmail.com
From: JacobCA@gmail.com
Subject: Re: Wow! What a surprise
Date: 4 August 00

It sound like you are getting a good first hand education of the socioeconomic conditions of the area.

How was Europe? I hope you have a better experience in Israel tomorrow.

The slow checkpoints occur because while maybe 98 or 99 of 100 Arabs are peaceful, if just one terrorist gets through he/she can kill dozens. The problem is not only the direct deaths and injured, but a suicide bomber also takes a psychological toll on those not directly affected. Some individuals will not venture outside because of fear. It slows commerce and interpersonal activities. So one terrorist can cause tremendous harm some of which is direct and apparent but in addition there is indirect harm which is not readily apparent. Hence the checkpoints are very thorough to make sure no one who shouldn't, passes through.

I am going to go to Boston and walk the Freedom Trail, something I always wanted to do. Then I will go to NY and spend a day or two since I leave from JFK.

Say "Hello" to Mom for me. I know she does not have a lap-top so I have not sent her any email.

Love, Jacob

To: JacobCA@gmail.com
From: JennyCA@gmail.com
Subject: Re: Wow! What a surprise
Date: 6 August 00

Good to hear from you; enjoy Boston and NY.

I feel great and they let me join Rashida's soccer team, I play a little. They are quite good, better ball handlers and passers than us in the United States. We have a game on 9 August but it will be done in time for us to cross the border to get to the bus station by 22:50. You will stay with your dad on the 9th. He knows that you are in the IDF and understands the situation; it won't be a problem. He is very grateful for what mom did years ago.

I understand the security issue. But I also can understand why the average non-militant Arab feels anger or hatred for Israel. The difference on each side of the border is striking. Israel has more than adequate food, utilities, transportation and job opportunities are at least adequate to good; on the Arab side, close to nonexistent.

Remember when we were in El Paso, we crossed over to see Juarez and how astounded we were of the great difference in how poor the people of Juarez were? The difference here is even more striking that between El Paso and Juarez. It's not just that there is a difference, but that difference is largely caused by Israel's actions. It seems that Israel is allowing the Arabs the minimal amount of resources to survive. If I were on the receiving end of that, I too would be resentful of those causing my misery.

For example, the Arabs really don't have sufficient water to irrigate that the Israelis have. Israelis both in Israel and in the West Bank are located in areas where the large aquifers are located. This provides them with ample water to grow olives and citrus. It's unfortunate that the Palestinian areas do not produce the same amount of water. Hence, there is little commerce and little wealth and almost no opportunity to get out of the situation.

I always used to wonder how two people could go some place or take a cruise and then describe it so differently. It is similar to seeing a vacation brochure with a beach with white clean sand, only a few people relaxing on blankets and no vendors. Then when you go there you realize the picture was of someone's private beach and the public beach is dirty with trash, crowded with tourists, no place to set down a blanket and very loud music which can't be seen on a brochure. Well now I understand how that happens. Someone could describe this place as poorer that Haiti or Juarez, with very difficult living conditions, limited utilities and limited water while others could describe upper middle class neighborhoods with plenty of water for swimming pools, etc. So much for my observations. You can see for yourself in less than a week.

We look forward to seeing you! Have a good trip.

Love, Jenny

On 9 August the soccer game was 1 to 1 when Amir and Sarah arrived at the 81st minute. Unfortunately, the other team scored in the 86th minute and Rashida's team lost. When the game ended, Amir looked at his watch. "I know it is only early afternoon but let's cross the border into Israel now so that will not become an issue later. We can then go to Jerusalem and, depending on when we get there, we may have some time to do some sightseeing before dinner. We need to be at the bus station before 22:50."

The four of them piled into Amir's 1992 Toyota and headed for the border crossing. Once there they crossed, and arrived at the Jerusalem bus station and parked in the municipal parking lot. Amir then informed the others, "This is the same bus station that Jacob's bus will arrive at. We have some time to see things. There are a few neat places within walking distance. After that, we can walk back and eat just two blocks from here. They have excellent gyros, something that we can not get in the West Bank. After dinner it will be just about a ten minute walk back to the bus station."

As they were finishing dinner Amir kept checking his watch and noted that it was nearing 22:30 so he suggested to the group that they begin to head towards the bus station. Just after they left and turned the corner to head towards the bus station, they heard a loud explosion from the direction of the bus station. Amir looked at his watch; it read 22:33.

"That explosion seemed near the bus station. However, it is only 22:34 and Jacob's bus does not arrive for another fifteen minutes. Buses in Israel are not always on time but very rarely are they early. So thankfully it was most likely something other than Bus 81. I need to get over there to see if they need the assistance of a physician. They even use us Arab doctors in emergencies."

Thirty-nine
BYE

"Eliz, how is Bob doing? . . . . Great. We are pleased that Bob is healing so well and he did not need chemo or radiation."

"Yes, we leave tomorrow and arrive on the 9th. Once we get to the hotel, we will email you that we are there."

Abraham's Tears

Vierzig
TAKE BUS #81

To: HBerniseWECB@gmail.com
From: GoldbergAD@gmail.com
Subject: Re: Our Meeting
Date: 8 August 00

Dr. Bernise:

Because of the late time on the 9th our driver will not be able to pick you up. Please take Bus #81 which leaves the airport at 20:00 and arrives in Jerusalem at 20:50. I will be at the bus station to meet you and take you to your hotel.

Our driver will pick your wife up on the 10th at TLV.

Aaron

Abraham's Tears

ארבעים ואחד/واحد وأربعون
Forty-one/Einundvierzig

TRAGEDY

Yazid, Jamil and Samira walked quickly towards the bus station. When they were within a block of the bus station they found the street and sidewalk was barricaded by two Israeli police officers who had just arrived and were beginning to secure the area. Yazid approached one of the officers and asked in Hebrew, "We are supposed to meet their mother who is on bus 81 at 22:50. Can we go thru to the bus station?" The officer used his radio to ask a question. After what seemed like an eternity of time, he received an answer and then responded. "You are correct. Bus 81 was due at 22:50. That bus brings passengers from Ben Gurion Airport to Jerusalem. Our operations department checked; no other buses were scheduled to arrive near that time. The explosion ahead was a bus at the bus station. It must have been bus 81 with passengers from the airport. But I can't let you thru now." "NO!" shrieked Jamil as Samira began to cry. Yazid quickly produced an identification card, "I am a surgical nurse and have helped with bombings before. These are my assistants, we would like to help." The officer looked as his fellow officer and then motioned them to pass.

Dr. Rahman followed by his daughter, Jenny and Sarah, made their way towards the bus station. As they came with in two blocks, they soon became enmeshed with police cars and ambulances all with lights and sirens going. As they came within a block of the bus station a police blockade prevented them from getting closer. Dr. Rahman inquired, "What happened?" The officer replied, "A suicide bomber struck as Bus 81 was disembarking." Dr. Rahman inquired, "Are you sure it was bus 81. It was not due until 22:50 and it is just 22:50 now." The officer quickly replied, "Yes, we checked. Since the bus was full, it left a few minutes early. You can't go past here." Before Dr. Rahman could respond Jenny yelled out, "Bus 81, that was the bus Jacob was on! No, no this can't happen to him." Jenny and Sarah looked at each other with eyes full of tears and tremblingly hugged each other. Dr. Rahman quickly responded, "I am Dr. Rahman, a physician, here is my identification as a physician. These people work with me." The officer then motioned them through. Sarah and Jenny looked at each other and Jenny shrieked,

As Aaron Goldberg was walking towards the bus station to meet Dr. Bernise when he heard the explosion. At that instant, given the place the explosion came from and its sound he knew what had unfortunately happened. Having lived his entire life in Israel, except for the five years of graduate school at MIT in Boston, he had become all too familiar with these murderous events. He quickly realized he needed to contact Dr. Bernise's wife and let her know what had happened. He obviously could not tell her that her husband was now in pieces spread all over the bus station along with pieces of Arabs, Israelis, Muslims, Jews, Christians and others on the bus. As he turned to walk back to his car, he was bewildered that the Islamic terrorists did not realize that when they committed these murderous attacks they just strengthened the resolve of those who had been attacked to defend Israel and Israelis. In addition, those in Israel who were sympathetic to Palestinian causes found it harder and harder to maintain an empathetic position rather than attack the Palestinians in retaliation.

As Yazid, Jamil and Samira reached the bus station, they could see the mangled bus ahead of them; part of it was still on fire. The three of them ran frantically towards the area of the burning bus, sidestepping the injured and dead as well as the bloody body parts torn from others. It was as if the area had been spray painted in blood. Everyone was screaming. The injured were in pain, others were wailing over the dead and medical workers yelling to get supplies or extra hands in treating the injured. As they were running Yazid yelled to them, "Stay very close to me. It is a favorite tactic of suicide bombers to work in pairs; the bombing of the bus may have been just to draw a crowd so a second bomber can set off another bomb which causes even more carnage. STAY CLOSE TO ME!" As they ran, Jamil noticed a familiar face. At first he could not place it; then it came to him. While Yazid and Samira ran towards the bus, Jamil moved to his right and yelled, "What are you doing here?

Mohammad quickly responded, "I didn't know there was a third."

Jamil's reflexive response was, "What third? I am with my brother and sister. I was supposed to meet my mother here at the bus station at 22:50."

Mohammad shot back, "Then you are not part of ...."

Jamil's mind immediately flashed back to one of the classes where it was taught that suicide bombers needed to work in pairs for the exact reasons Yazid had stated a minute earlier. As Mohammad began to move forward, Jamil's eyes quickly dropped down to Mohammad's vest area and widened in horror. Jamil quickly recognized that under Mohammad's oversized jacket were the chemicals of death. Jamil defensively responded, "Oh, no! No! Please, my mother is dead. Please, please that is my only family left." Without thinking Jamil jumped on Mohammad to prevent him from moving towards his remaining family.

As Dr. Rahman, Sarah, Jenny and Rashida reached the area of where the dead and the injured lay, Sarah noticed one young man the same size as Jacob who she could not see well since his back was turned to her, jump another and attempting to take him to the ground. Hoping her son had disembarked from the bus before the explosion, she reflexively moved to help her son.

Jamil and Mohammad wrestled a second or two before Jamil took them both to the ground an instant before a blast shredded both their young bodies and many others, including Sarah, but many fewer than would have been murdered had Jamil not acted.

Dr. Rahman realizing a second suicide bomber had hit, grabbed Jenny and Rashida and pulled them away.

The minute Samira saw Jamil attack the stranger she began moving trying to help her brother. The blast knocked her to the ground. She got up with blood coming from a number of wounds where the bomb's projectiles had hit. She started to run towards where Jamil had given his life to save hers, but Yazid's two big arms quickly grabbed her and pulled her close. "There is nothing you or I can do right now for him and there may be yet another bomber. You need to stay away. I am very, very sorry. You have lost your only brother and I have lost my only family." Sobbing and clinging to someone she was not related to, and had just met a couple of weeks ago, was Samira, a young Muslim woman who had lost her only family, the two people who meant the most to her, screaming, "The killing has got to stop. THIS CRAZINESS HAS GOT TO END."

Across the blood-stained area littered with body parts and with the remains of the mangled bus still on fire stood a Arab/Muslim physician with Jenny, a young Jewish woman pounding on him while screaming, "The killing has got to stop. THIS CRAZINESS HAS GOT TO END."

As Pastor Fitzgerald was watching BBC News he was horrified to hear of the suicide bombing in Jerusalem of Bus 81 which the Doerr family was taking from the airport to Jerusalem to begin their tour. As he was dialing Elizabeth Dodson, he was thinking to himself at times like this Abraham must be crying.

Abraham's Tears

خاتمة/אפילוג
EPILOGUE/EPILOG

The University of Michigan
School of Middle East Studies
12 March 2001
Program: OneVoice - Group Discussion

Ladies and gentlemen, our presenter tonight is Ms. Lynn Tucker of OneVoice, please welcome her

[courteous applause for Ms. Tucker].

"OneVoice's usual program is a presentation by a Palestinian/Muslim and an Israeli/Jew. They discuss their lives in the Middle East and explain why they have joined OneVoice in an attempt to end violence and bring peace to the Middle East. In addition, they explain how they plan to do so - by getting Israelis and Palestinians to know each other and to settle any differences by negotiations rather than war. However, tonight our program will not involve speakers from the Middle East, but rather will involve you. We have decided to do this because of the large number of students attending the University of Michigan are from the Middle East as well as the large Muslim and Jewish communities of greater Detroit."

"I would like to get a better feeling of your connection to the Middle East, both in the past and present."

"How many of you were born in the Middle East? Wow, about half of you. How many of you still have relatives there? About the same number."

"How many of you have been in the Middle East at least twice during the past five years? About 30 or 40 of you."

"How many of you during the past year have followed the Middle East situation not from the United States news, but from news from the Middle East, either newspaper, TV, Internet or friends/relatives that live there? Wow, maybe 80 or 90% of you. Excellent. About half of you have first-hand experience with the Middle East and many of the others follow what is going on, not only from U.S. news but seek out how others report on the situation. We should have a very interesting program."

"I especially would like to hear from those of you who have lived anywhere in the Middle East for a period of time and have an idea as to how best to resolve the situation so Arabs/Muslims and Israelis/Jews can live peacefully together."

A few hands were raised.

"The gentlemen at the back."

"I am an Arab from Lebanon. I think you have over-simplified the situation as being between two parties. In reality there are the Arab/Muslim 'Joe citizens' who are merchants, farmers and laborers who could live and work very well next to an Israeli/Jew. Similarly many Israelis/Jews could live and work next to Arab/Muslims. Proof of this is that many Arab/Muslims live and work peacefully in Israel including Arabs who have been on the Israeli Supreme Court. The third group is the 'activist' Arab/Muslims which would include Hamas, Hezbollah and others who do not want peace with Israel, but want to eliminate it. Because of their violent means, Israel has taken actions protective of Israel which have put a vice-like grip on Arabs so severe that it limits their ability to do business and live reasonably. However, because Hamas and Hezbollah are smart enough to provide important social quasi-governmental services to the Arab population, the average Arab will not speak out against any actions of Hamas or Hezbollah. Further, may are afraid to do so because of retaliation. If the Arab middle, who can live with Israel, speaks out for peace, I believe we will have a two state solution. However, that will not happen until some group can (1) provide these people with the services that Hamas and Hezbollah are providing and (2) protect the Arab population from retribution from these militant groups."

"Thank you. That is an excellent and realistic summary of the situation. OneVoice has not dealt with either of these militant groups because they are not interested in peace. The gentleman over here in front with the Detroit Red Wings sweatshirt."

"I am an Arab from Egypt and I concur with the previous speaker. Another way to view the situation is to look to see how Iranians have responded to their president's absurd denial of the Holocaust and his advocating the destruction of Israel. If they agreed with him, they would have shouted out in support. Yet most are quiet. Why quiet? Because they disagree, but are afraid to speak out and condemn their leader. It is well known what happens to those in Iran who speak out against the government. Similarly, it is known what will happen to those who oppose Hamas or Hezbollah's position regarding Israel."

"Has anyone in the audience lost a close relative, parent, child, brother, sister, etc to the fighting? I would like to hear your perspective...The lady with the blue and white blouse.

"My brother and I were born in Israel and our family is Jewish. Our father and my aunt were killed there in an ambush by Palestinians when we were very young. After dad was killed, my mother moved our family to Los Angeles to escape the warfare. My brother became a member of the IDF. My mother and I were in Jerusalem last summer and were to meet my brother on 9 August. He was flying to Israel and was taking a bus from the airport to join us in Jerusalem. When we went to pick him up at the bus station a suicide bomber destroyed the bus and killed my brother. A second suicide bomber killed my mother. I have lost my entire family, mother, father and brother to these crazy murders. These killings and reprisal killings have gone on since the creation of Israel in 1948. Half a century of killings has solved nothing. This craziness has to stop. I don't want revenge; I don't want an Arab killed as a reprisal. I just want peace."

"I am very sorry to hear about your numerous losses. Your not seeking revenge will greatly aid the peace process. The woman in the middle with the University of Michigan sweat shirt.

"I am speechless. Before the last speaker, I knew what I was going to say. Now I don't know where to begin. My mother, an Arab-Muslim, was on the same bus on 9 August as the previous speaker's Jewish brother. My brother and I were at the bus stop awaiting her arrival. The second suicide bomber killed my brother as he did her mother. I offer my condolences to her for her loss. In my situation, both my mother and brother were killed by my Arab 'brothers'. That does not make the pain any less than if they had been killed by Israelis. I too had come here to plead for an end to killing. It never ends. She and I have each lost our parents and brothers. Please, please stop the killing. I now attend the University of Michigan here in Ann Arbor and have noticed that in the Detroit area there are large Muslim and Jewish populations. I don't remember hearing of any problem between these two groups. We are all children of Abraham. There is no reason why we can not live the same way in the Middle East. If the Israeli woman who lost her mother and brother would be willing to meet with me, I would like to talk to her. Maybe we can work together to stop this senseless killing."

"I would be most willing to meet with you and anyone else who is willing to stop the killing and work for peace. Unfortunately, this situation which has not benefited either side has gone on for over half a century. This Craziness Has Got To End."

دموع إبراهيم

דמעות של אברהם

Abraham's Tears

ACKNOWLEDGMENTS

The author would like to thank all of those who read various drafts or parts of this novel and provided invaluable suggestions for improving it, in particular Professor Judah Ari-Gur, Rabbi Harvey Spivak, David Stein, Professor Mustafa Mughazy, Professor Amy Baily, Maher Awad and Jen Nails.

In addition, the author would like to thank Ellen Nelson for her front cover concept and Jarron Bowman for spending hours discussing, reading, providing invaluable comments including the encouragement to continue on this endeavor for which I was neither trained nor experienced.

Further, the author would like to thank the Student Muslim Association at Western Michigan University for providing critical information regarding an explanation of the Qur'an for those of us in the Western world who otherwise would not have learned what the Qur'an says.

Abraham's Tears

AUTHOR'S NOTE

This is a novel; none of the characters[1] or activities has any connection to any real person or event. To the extent that any of them do, it is purely by coincidence and unknown to the author.

I have tried to not offend anyone of religious faith, particularly Christians, Jews and Muslims. If I have said something for which the reader takes offense, please know it is by inadvertence or ignorance and accept my apology.

With no intent to offend anyone, my goal is to get various ethnic and religious parties to realize that we should travel the same way on the highway of peace rather than opposite ways on the divided highway of war. The tragic tit-for-tat killings in the Middle East should be replaced by a negotiated peaceful situation so all can live in peace and dignity in such a historic and beautiful place. As Mohandas Gandas said, "An eye for an eye only ends up making the whole world blind."

---

1. Cardinal Jean-Marie Lustiger and Israeli Supreme Court Justices Abdel Rahman Zuabi and Salim Joubran, both Arabs, are real individuals and the information about them is factually correct.

The people of the Middle East deserve better than to spend their time, resources and lives involved in retaliatory killings.

With regard to the causative factor of the Middle East violence over the land which is Israel and the Palestinian Territories, the common view is that it is a religious dispute between Jews and Muslims. I respectfully dissent. My reasons for dissenting are set forth in the chapter, twenty-five, Israel Arab Conflict – Answer. That chapter shows the conflict over Israel/Palestine is not a religious one between Islam and Judaism or an ethnic one between Arabs and Israelis. If the Israelis had sold Israel and the holy places to the non-religious Chinese, and then left the area to the Chinese, the Arabs/Muslims would have no conflict with Israelis/Jews. Their new enemy would be the Chinese.

Assume United Nations Resolution 181 in 1948 gave the land now called Israel, including the religious places, to left-handed individuals of all religions and ethnic groups which then had full control. Would right-handed Muslims be "at war" with the left handers? Would right handed Jews be "at war" with the left handers? Might the right-handed Muslims and right-handed Jews combine efforts against the left handers who would be controlling the land they believed to be theirs? I think so.

The primary reason for the conflict is that there is only one piece of land, Jerusalem (including its holy places) that two parties claim. It is just chance that the owners and the non-owners of the land have different religions and of different ethnicities.

If I am correct, the importance is then the solution to the Middle East conflict is easier.

Years ago because I was an attorney involved in negotiating patent licenses, I read *Getting To Yes* (a book about negotiating). In the book there is an example of two sisters fighting over a lemon. It was decided to cut it in half and give half to each sister. One sister peeled the lemon, threw away the rind and used the pulp. The other peeled the lemon, threw away the pulp and used the rind. A creative solution of separating the lemon pulp from the rind and then giving the entire rind to one sister and the entire pulp to the other would have been better for both sisters. While it will take more creativity than solving the lemon problem, I believe the Middle East issues can be solved *IF* both parties are really interested in reaching an agreement on a two-state solution that is good for both parties.

Some method of sharing seems to be the best way to handle the fact that there is only one Old Jerusalem, one Temple Mount and one Tomb of the Patriarchs, etc wanted by different groups. If title to all the holy places was given to Abraham and his heirs, the issues of ownership would be solved. It would still leave the most crucial and practical problem of administration. If two groups of people of faith can't work out how to administer rather small amounts of property together, how can they ever work out how to manage two countries side by side together in peace? The details of how such sharing can best be done is beyond the scope of this book. But hopefully this book may stimulate reasonable people on both sides to realize that the answer is to find some way of peacefully sharing the holy land rather than continuing the warfare that has changed little over the past half century while causing many deaths, much suffering and little peace.

While I don't believe the primary cause of the Middle East conflict is religious differences, nevertheless religious differences are in the forefront and must be dealt with.

The teachings of the good book of most religions are similar, containing the outlines of the Golden Rule and the items set forth in the Ten Commandments. They are also the nexus of many of the world's problems. In Northern Ireland two Christian groups, Catholics and Protestants, murdered each other for years in the name of their respective religions. More recently, in Iraq two Muslim groups, the Sunni and Shiite, have been brutally killing each other. In the Middle East, it is the Muslims and Jews.

There are religious people who believe deeply but know that all religious beliefs are just that, beliefs. While they think theirs is the only correct and true religion, they acknowledge that others will believe similarly of their religions. Because of this understanding, those individuals can practice their own religion and respect their neighbors who practice a different religion (or no religion); live and let live. If we all follow the rules of our own good book, we should live peacefully side by side. In the Middle East, and elsewhere, many of these enlightened individuals are involved in the excellent group, OneVoice, which is a grassroots organization of Palestinians and Israelis committed to a peaceful solution to the Middle East problems where Arabs and Israelis, Muslims and Jews can live side by side with Christians and others.

However, there are others of all religions who believe that their religion is the only correct and true religion and therefore want to impose their beliefs and practices on others. This is an excellent time-tested recipe for bitter conflict and war. History shows that. No one wants to have the religious beliefs of others forced on them directly or indirectly.

I believe that how one views the Palestinian-Israeli situation depends primarily on the views that one was exposed to during one's developmental years.

Author's Note

There is no Christian, Jewish, or Muslim gene that programs one to follow a particular "true god-given" religion. Assume a rabbi's wife and an imam's wife were giving birth in the same hospital on the same day to baby boys and the babies were inadvertently switched. The birth son of the imam raised by the rabbi's family would grow up reading Hebrew not Arabic, being Bar Mitzvah wearing a tallis for prayer, believing the two most important religious holidays are Yom Kippur and Passover and thinking Mecca had no religious significance. Similarly, the birth son of the rabbi, raised by the imam's family would not believe in wearing a yarmulke for prayer, he would read Arabic not Hebrew, he would pray five times a day to Allah rather than morning and evening, celebrate Ramadan and not Yom Kippur and believe Mecca is one of the holiest cities in the world. An excellent real world situation that proves this is Cardinal Jean-Marie Lustiger. He was born Jewish, converted to Catholicism and eventually became a Cardinal in the Catholic Church. In this novel, Jacob who was Bar Mitzvah finds out he was born a Muslim.

So there is no religious gene which gives us the correct religious programming or education for "the true religion". There is no absolute right or wrong with regard to religious issues; it is what we are taught and learn in our religious education. If we can get people of various religions to walk around the table of religious issues and see the issues from the other side, hopefully the observer would realize that it is all a matter of perspective. That being the situation, then it is possible to educate religious individuals, not to give up their beliefs, but to realize that the religious beliefs of others are as legitimate as theirs. When they do that, they will then respect others for following their religious beliefs. Religious people who respect the religious beliefs of other religions, can sit at that same table and discuss their differences and how to cooperate instead of planning the destruction of "the enemy".

From my experience participating in public program discussions of Middle East issues, one thing immediately became crystal clear — that these discussions almost always led to retrospective incrimination of the actions and misdeeds of the other side followed by blame based on those activities. Little can be done about the past, but we can take actions regarding the future. There is no question that people on both sides of the fence can make out what they believe is an excellent case for their position, and both sides can find abuses and misdeeds of the other. Arguing historical or religious points that the other side does not accept, will not move the process forward; there is not a universal judge here on earth who has the authority to say which side is correct and what the remedy should be. Blaming the other side based on retrospective activities does not move the process along. Quite the contrary, those who were criticized or blamed quickly dig in their heels and find things to blame the other side for.

What I have found that works extremely well is to require those involved in arguing/discussing these problems to only discuss issues prospectively. For example, some have pointed out that when discussing issues like prisoners one must look back as to why or how they were taken. Not so, that loops into the blame game. The way to approach that type of an issue is to ask, how are we going to solve the situation of the prisoners that is satisfactory to both sides? That is something that reasonable people can discuss and do something about in a way that facilitates the peace process.

Author's Note

I am sure some readers will doubt the ability of individuals, on either side in the Middle East, who have lost loved ones or who have suffered grave injustices at the hands of the "enemy" to look past the loss, not retaliate and work for peace. While the scenario in the Epilogue is fiction; it is realistic. In fact while writing this Author's Note, two news reports described situations where this was actually occurring.

On September 11th, 2001, Mark Stroman lost his sister in the World Trade Center while he was at home watching the nightmare on TV. Just 10 days after the attacks of Sept. 11, 2001, Rais Bhuiyan was working at a gas station in Dallas when he was shot in the face by Mark Stroman. Stroman was on a shooting spree, targeting and killing people who appeared to be Muslim or of Middle Eastern descent. Stroman was arrested, tried, convicted and scheduled to be executed July 20, 2011 in Texas. Bhuiyan, who is the only survivor of Stroman's vicious attacks, fought to save Stroman's life.

Bhuiyan had to go through several painful surgeries during the past decade, lost his vision in one eye and is still carrying more than 35 pellets on the right side of his face. Yet Bhuiyan instead of supporting the execution of Stroman, tried to save Stroman's life. He did so because according to him, in Islam, there is no hate and no killing. He says, "Yes, Mark Stroman did a horrible thing, and he brought a lot of pain and disaster, sufferings in my life. But in return I never hated him."

Bhuiyan strongly believes that executing Stroman is not a solution. He says, "We will just simply lose a human life without dealing with the root cause, which is hate crime. In Islam it says that saving one human life is the same as saving the entire mankind. Since I forgave him, all those principles encouraged me to go even further, and stop his execution and save another human life." Stroman was executed by the State of Texas on 20 July 2011.

If Bhuiyan who unjustly suffered so much at the hands of Stroman, did not seek retaliatory revenge then certainly the rest of us, who have not suffered as Bhuiyan did, should be able to seek peace rather than blood.

On 31 July 2011 the Guardian reported that an Iranian woman, Ameneh Bahrami, blinded by an acid attack pardoned her assailant as he faced the same fate as ordered by an Iranian Court. The victim under Iranian law could vacate the court's order by pardoning the defendant. She withdrew the 'eye for an eye' retribution hours before surgeons were prepared to blind her attacker in one eye with acid. Her attacker threw acid in her face because she would not marry him. The acid both blinded and disfigured her.

These are two powerful examples of individual who were wronged but did not seek retribution but instead forgave the attacker. We are more likely to have peace if the world will learn from people like this.

Hopefully, more knowledge and respect for each other will bring more understanding which in turn will lead us to find a way to live together in peace, even with those whom we do not always agree.

Bruce Stein

CPSIA information can be obtained at www.ICGtesting.com
Printed in the USA
BVOW080723210812

298410BV00001B/1/P